monsoonbooks

INSIDE THE HOUSE OF THE RAJA

Author and photographer Xavier Comas is a fine arts graduate of the University of Barcelona, whose work has been published and exhibited in Europe and Asia, as well as being featured by prominent magazines throughout the world. The Singapore Art Museum exhibited his installation *Pasajero* in 2009 and acquired his *Jiutamai* series as a permanent collection. In researching *The House of the Raja*, Comas immersed himself in the Deep South of Thailand for over a year and returns regularly.

T0169089

XAVIER COMAS

INSIDE THE HOUSE OF THE RAJA

My journey to a forgotten palace
in Thailand's troubled Deep South

monsoon

monsoonbooks

Published in 2018
by Monsoon Books Ltd
www.monsoonbooks.co.uk

No.1 Duke of Windsor Suite, Burrough Court,
Burrough on the Hill, Leicestershire LE14 2QS, UK

Part of the text first published in an illustrated book
"The House of the Raja" by Xavier Comas (River Books Press, 2014)

ISBN (paperback): 9781912049387
ISBN (ebook): 9781912049394

Copyright©Xavier Comas, 2014
The moral right of the author has been asserted.

All rights reserved. No part of this publication may be reproduced,
stored in a retrieval system, or transmitted, in any form or by any means
without the prior written permission of the publisher, nor be otherwise
circulated in any form of binding or cover other than that in which
it is published and without a similar condition being imposed on the
subsequent purchaser.

Cover design by Cover Kitchen.

A Cataloguing-in-Publication data record is available from the British
Library.

Printed and bound in Great Britain by Clays Ltd, Elcograf S.p.A.
20 19 18   1 2 3 4 5

CERITA	STORY

di suatu senja
di kaki gunung
di bibir tasik
sewaktu menghayun kaki
ayah pun bercerita:
"Nak! di sini dahulu
pada suatu masa
ada seorang raja bertakhta
ada sebuah kubah beriman
ada sebidang taman berpendekar
anak-anak bersorak ria
di bawah mentari segar
dan bulan bersinar..."
anak pun bertanya:
"Ayah! tapi sekarang di mana?"
ayah melihat jauh
ke hujung ufuk
kemudian membenan mukanya
ke dasar tasik yang hitam.

as dusk fell
at the foot of a mountain
on the shore of a lake
while walking
father told a story:
"My son! In this place
once upon a time
there was a king on the throne
there was a dome of faith
there was a garden of warriors
children were joyfully playing
under the fresh sunlight
and the bright moonlight..."
son asked his father:
"Father! but where are they now?"
father gazed
at the end of the horizon
then sank his face
in the bottom of the black lake.

An anonymous poem from an anthology compiled by a group of Patani Malay writers called **ASIP (Angkatan Sasterawan/Penulis Melayu Patani)**

Translated by **Hara Shintaro**

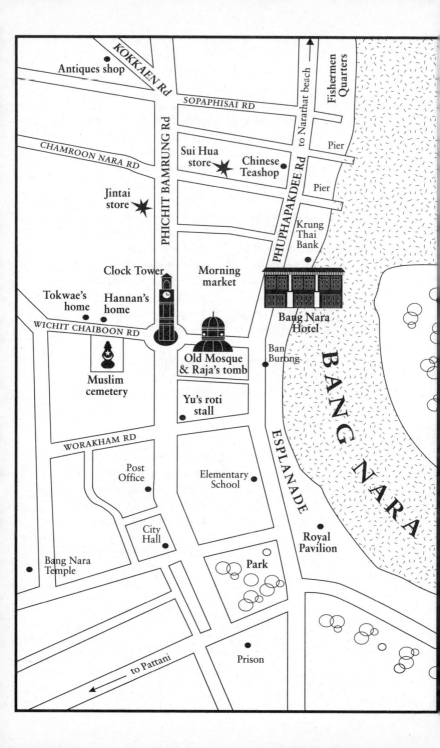

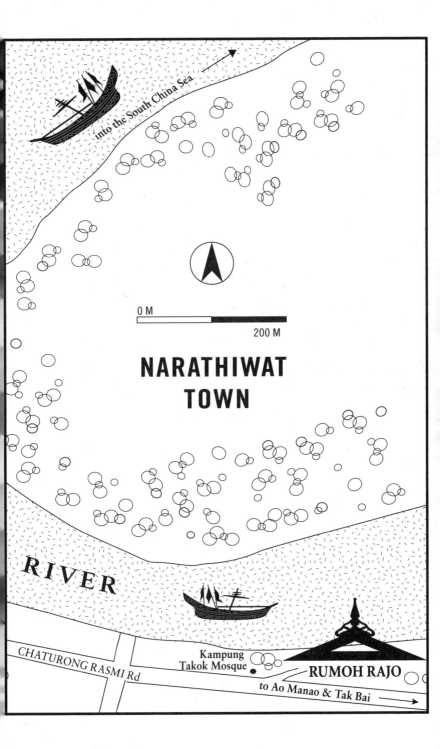

INTRODUCTION

Standing in an Islamic school in Narathiwat, the southernmost province of Thailand, my gaze falls upon a time-worn book inside a glass cabinet. After requesting a closer look, the caretaker removes the book slowly and presents it to me saying, "Be very careful. It's a rare piece."

I caress the ragged surface of its black, leathery cover with the tips of my fingers before opening it. Pages unfold to reveal delicate coloured patterns and Arabic script bearing witness to centuries of history. To my amazement, the man says it is an 800-year-old parchment Qur'an from Al-Andalus, the ancient Moorish Kingdom in the south of modern-day Spain. By a quirk of fate, I know Al-Andalus, today called Andalusia, as it is my mother's homeland. Now, in a forgotten corner of Asia far away from Andalusia, I can't believe I'm holding one of its treasures in my hands.

During my youth, I had viewed that southern land with

contempt, partly because of my mixed heritage – a *xarnego*[1], born in Barcelona, capital of Catalonia, to a proud Catalan father and an Andalusian mother. Our Sunday visits to my grandparents in a neighbourhood of southern immigrants and gypsies were the only contact with my maternal roots. Andalusia remained in my mind a foreign, poor corner of dry land with olive trees and day labourers. It was only a trip there a few years ago that finally caused my Andalusian blood to stir.

The climax of my visit was the Moorish Palace of Alhambra, wandering amidst the finest Islamic artistry the world has ever known; Arabesques, Quranic verses and poems run along its floors and walls, whirling round columns up to vaulted ceilings, arches and window frames, turning the pages of a faerie book written in stone. But what touched me the most was the atemporal atmosphere in those spaces, still breathing with memories and whispers of its vanquished kingdom. The experience left me craving for more of its history and my roots.

Hundreds of years of warfare between Al-Andalus and the Iberian Christian kingdoms drew Muslim scholars and merchants to more auspicious Eastern lands. Civil war and the breakup into a number of petty kingdoms led Al-Andalus to gradual decline

---

1 *Xarnego* – or *charnego*, its equivalent in Spanish – is a pejorative Catalan word that refers to a person's identity. Coined during the 1950s-70s in the Catalonia region of Spain to denote a working-class person who immigrated from Southern Spain (typically due to a depressed economy in their place of origin) and did not speak or learn Catalan, the primary language spoken in the region and one of Spain's four official languages. Nowadays, a *xarnego* is a derogatory term for someone born in Catalonia with immigrant or mixed heritage, particularly Andalusian.

until the *Reconquista* came to fruition with the surrender of the Emirate of Granada at the gates of Alhambra, the final bastion of Islam in Western Europe. As the last Moorish Kingdom vanished from Spain, another Islamic realm took hold and began to flourish in the Far East: the Malay Kingdom of Patani. Twilight and dawn of these two Muslim Kingdoms are bound by the invisible strands of history.

In time, Patani blossomed as a major regional emporium, frequented by Chinese, Arabs, Persians, Siamese, Japanese and Europeans who settled there and exchanged goods, technology and ideas. Today, Thailand's three southernmost provinces encompass part of this erstwhile kingdom: Pattani, Yala and Narathiwat.

Both Al-Andalus and Patani are romanticised lands that evoke a wistful past in which an amalgam of different cultures and religions flourished together, leaving a profound and long-lived impact in their respective regions. Both Al-Andalus and Patani were peninsular kingdoms at a crossroads between worlds: the former a border between Islam and Christianity, a fulcrum of trade between East and West; the latter, a frontier between Malay-Muslims and Thai-Buddhists, a commercial link between India and China and confluence between the Near East and Indochina. Both achieved literary and artistic heights with the adoption of Arabic as the script of their vernacular languages, the Mozarabic of the Andalusians and the Jawi of the Malays. Now, both southern lands are poor and underdeveloped compared to other regions in their own countries.

While the grandeur of Al-Andalus lives on in its palaces

today, fading memories are the sole legacy of Patani, even though its great history takes us further back into the past, to a time long before the advent of Islam in the world.

Imagine a kingdom at the time of the Pax Romana, on a far-flung Asian peninsula called the 'Land of Gold', a realm of spirits and magic blessed by Hindu gods, a kingdom founded by a prince, who, according to legend, was descended from Alexander the Great. This fabled land was called Langkasuka. It spanned the Malay Peninsula with ports on the west and east coasts that linked the maritime silk route for centuries.

Roman, Persian, Indian and Chinese envoys, merchants and adventurers, Brahmin and Buddhist missionaries, all sailed the treacherous waters of the Andaman and South China seas to reach this El Dorado of the East. Coveted by every empire in Southeast Asia over a millennium, Langkasuka was shaped by a tapestry of civilisations and beliefs that mingled with the existing animism. Later, with the rise and fall of the kingdoms and dynasties to which it eventually paid tribute, its name also changed. Yet, Langkasuka prevailed as an ethos of a land, its culture and its people, the Melayu.

Sometime after the 13th century, Langkasuka vanished mysteriously from history, its name lost to mythology and its ethos bequeathed to its heir, the Malay Kingdom of Patani, founded by a Hindu-Buddhist king of the Sri Wangsa dynasty whose descendants converted to Islam. Patani soon became a beacon of Malay culture and a major trade entrepôt.

In hindsight, the rise of Patani came as a result of a chain of events in fifteenth-century Spain, in a year that would shape the emergence of the first-ever global market and the beginning of our 'modern' world: 1492.

That within this same year the expulsion of the Jews and the conquest of the Emirate of Granada preceded the discovery of the New World, was not a mere coincidence. All three events are interconnected, for the wealth confiscated by the Catholic kings from Jews and Muslims provided for Columbus' expedition. In fact, not only was the explorer present when Muhammad XII, the last ruler of Al-Andalus, surrendered the key of Granada to King Ferdinand and Queen Isabella, but he was in the Hall of the Ambassadors of the Alhambra palace, under dazzling Islamic carvings with the Nasrid dynasty motto, "There is no victor but Allah", where the edict expelling the Jews was signed and Columbus received royal endorsement for his voyage. It was a voyage that would decide the destiny of Asia and the rise of Patani as the jewel of the Indochina seas.

In the wake of the fall of Constantinople under the Ottomans in 1453, Arabs had become the gatekeepers of the spice trade, barring Western Europe from its access through the ancient Silk Road, so Europeans set out to find alternative routes by sea. Portugal sent its galleons along the coast of Africa, trying to find a way to the Indic sea, while Columbus convinced Spain of a shortcut to India by rounding the earth sailing West.

Upon Columbus' return from his first grueling voyage, the Portuguese king sent a threatening letter to the Catholic monarchs claiming the discovered lands. With no military power in the

Atlantic to match the Portuguese, the Catholic monarchs pursued a diplomatic negotiation.

Only the voice of God on earth could decide over the rule of kings, so Pope Alexander VI decreed in a series of bulls that divided the non-Christian world in two. What lay to the west would belong to Spain and what lay to the east went to Portugal. Only after the completion of these negotiations with Spain would Vasco de Gama accomplish the first direct trip from Europe to Asia, rounding the Cape of Good Hope at the southern tip of Africa. When he came ashore in Calicut, he inaugurated a long campaign of brilliant naval strategies against tremendous odds to wrest control of the spice trade from Muslim traders. King Manuel I of Portugal pursued a monopoly of all sea lanes in the Indic Ocean, an enterprise to become the first empire in world history of global dimensions, culminating in 1511 with the conquest of a key port that controlled trade with China: the Sultanate of Malacca.

When the Sultan of Malacca sent for help to the Ming emperor of China against the Portuguese, the emperor ordered his tributary, the Ayutthaya Kingdom, to come to Malacca's aid. But the Siamese king, who had tried to invade Malacca himself a few years earlier, naturally refused to comply.

The Portuguese soon realised that their capture of Malacca diverted commerce to other ports in the region. Patani, blessed with a bay sheltered from monsoon storms and a welcoming ruler, bloomed throughout the sixteenth century as a major producer of gold, pepper, ivory, sandalwood, precious stones and the deerskin that dressed samurais. From China and Japan came white and yellow silk, damasks, gauzes, satins, porcelain, iron and copper. Traders from both sides of the peninsula made use of overland and fluvial routes that connected Patani with the Indian Ocean.

The shift in trade also brought a massive influx of Islamic merchants, who linked the sultanate into wider networks that stretched as far as south as Sulawesi. But the rise of the "door to China and Japan", as Patani would be called, was not to come without a price.

This was a time when Southeast Asian countries existed as centres of power that radiated outwards from omnipotent sovereigns, often overlapping circumjacent powers. In the West, kings ruled by the grace of God, but, in the Orient, gods themselves ruled on earth a numinous world in the image and likeness of the heavens. Politics meant personal relationships between emperors, kings and overlords, and vassalage status fluctuated accordingly, for all Imperial China kept preeminence as the centre of this celestial order for two millennia. Siam paid homage to the Chinese emperor, and in turn, Patani paid tribute to the former. In much the same way Nasrid emirs in Granada paid tribute to Castilian kings in gold dinars, Patani also paid tribute to Siam, albeit in the quainter and more artful form of a tree bloomed with flowers and birds perched on its branches, all sculpted in gold, called the *Bunga Mas*. Every three years, the Raja of Patani presented the golden tree to the king of Ayutthaya, considered by the Malay rajas as a token of friendship, but deemed by the Siamese kings as homage paid to their incontestable supremacy.

At the end of the 16th century, four successive queens, named after the colours of the rainbow, brought Patani to its golden age. They constructed a number of canals to provide the growing population with fresh water and allow transportation of goods within the city and to more distant docks. Fearing an attack from an increasingly aggressive and desirous Ayutthaya, the Blue Queen commissioned mighty brass cannons to defend Patani's royal citadel. Her successor, the Purple Queen, refused to send the Bunga Mas, after the usurpation by Prasat Thong of the throne in Ayuthaya. The virulent response was swift. Still, the queens managed to repel four major Siamese invasions, but war brought political disorder, together with a contraction in trade. Finally, the end of the queenly lineage sealed its fate and the first Siamese king of the Chakri dynasty razed a weakened Patani to the ground in 1786. Two months after the downfall, the massive wooden structure of the Raja's palace was still smoldering. People were carried off in such large numbers that the country was almost completely depopulated.

Sir Francis Light, the founder of Penang, described in a letter the atrocities by the Siamese army: "... all the men, children and old women being tied and thrown upon the ground and then trampled to death by elephants." More than 4,000 men were taken away as slaves to build the new capital of Siam, Bangkok. During the 19th century, Siamese soldiers journeyed south again to crush Malay uprisings and to provide further slave labour that was resettled along the canals of Bangkok, where their descendants still live today.

The Siamese king appointed a puppet raja to increasingly

dominate and absorb Patani, feeding a deep resentment among the Malays. Siam never strengthened the position of tributary Malay rulers by the help of their own countrymen but rather fostered dissension among their household. Whilst Siamese control over Kelantan was relative and even weaker on Terengannu, they could exert their divisive policy in full with Patani after its military defeat. Five decades of wars and uprisings followed, prompting Siam to adopt a 'divide and rule' policy. In 1817, Patani was carved up into seven small kingdoms that had traditionally been an integral part of a greater Patani, each ruled by an appointed raja who continued dispatching the Bunga Mas to the Siamese monarchs. If a raja proved troublesome, he would be promptly dislodged and replaced with a subservient next of kin.

After the Anglo-Siamese Treaty of 1909, King Rama V relinquished claims to his vassal Malay states and forcibly annexed the Seven Malay Principalities first as a county called Monthon Pattani[2] and later as three provinces: Yala, Pattani and Narathiwat. During the territorial administrative reform to create a united centralised Siam, Bangkok began acting like a colonial power towards its former tributary kingdoms, and later assimilated them to forge a modern nation-state, Thailand.

As government officials displaced indigenous elites in administrative positions, the local population grew in agitation.

---

2 The *monthon* was a bureaucratic administrative system introduced in 1897 by the first Siamese Minister of Interior, Prince Damrong Rajanubhab, marking the transition from the old tributary system to the administrative division of Siam that formed the basis of modern Thailand.

A prophecy dating back to the days of King Rama I, which predicted the end of the Chakri dynasty on its 150th anniversary, became a sudden reality on June 24, 1932, when a bloodless coup d'état, engineered by a political group of civil servants and army officers, put an end to 800 years of absolute rule by Siamese kings. The ideologue of the coup, Pridi Banomyong, became estranged from the leader of the military faction, Field Marshal Plaek Phibunsongkhram, who soon manoeuvred to seize his seat as the premier. An admirer of the Europe of Hitler and Mussolini, Phibunsongkhram set himself as the first of the numerous dictators obsessed with 'modernising' Thailand until today. The leader established a ministry of propaganda under Luang Wichitwathakan, the architect of Thainess and the change of Siam to Thailand. Following the fascist playbook, he launched a cultural totalitarian purification that was to civilise the country, uplift the national spirit and promote moral values in such a sweeping way that the Generalissimo himself in Francoist Spain would have been envious.

Far from fulfilling hopes for freedom upon the fall of absolutism, Bangkok's policies persecuted those Malay-Muslims in the south whose cultural identity clashed with the Thai credo. The Malay language, once the lingua franca in the court of Ayutthaya and all Southeast Asia, was banned together with Malay customs, traditional attire and Islamic family laws.

As many dictators do, the Field Marshal was preoccupied with trivialities that attracted popular criticism, and while he endeavoured in nation-building by forcing the people to wear hats or imposing pad Thai as the national dish, World War II loomed in Asia. Shortly after the Japanese invasion, Phibunsongkhram signed a military alliance with Japan in return for its southern Malay dependencies, previously lost to Britain. Much of the prevailing militarism in Thailand derives from the Japanese martial code of *bushido*. The son of the last Raja of Patani, Tengku Mahmud Mahyuddin, assisted the British by launching guerilla attacks against the Japanese forces in a deal that promised independence from Thailand if the Allies were victorious. The British, originally eager to punish the Thai government for aiding the Japanese conquest of Malaya, backtracked on their promise at the insistence of the United States, who needed Thailand as a staunch ally to deter the impending communist menace in Asia.

With the rajas and the Malay aristocracy long gone, the struggle against subjugation was now led by commoners. Haji Sulong, a Malay scholar and advocate of a modernist Islam who was dissatisfied with the forced assimilation of his people, put forward a petition that called for autonomy, language and cultural rights, and the restoration of Islamic family and inheritance law. Sulong also sent a letter to Tengku Mahmud Mahyuddin inviting him to represent the Malay community in their appeal. In the paranoiac eyes of the authorities, this amounted to an offense of sedition and Sulong was arrested. In 1948, a petition to the newly established United Nations was signed by some 250,000 Malay Muslims to seek accession of the three provinces to the Federated States of Malaya. The Phibun government apprehended many of the signatories and the petition had no effect whatsoever. In

April that year, insurrection erupted, reportedly killing five police officers, while hundreds of Malays, including women, children and elders lost their lives. A few years later, Sulong disappeared under suspicious circumstances, presumably murdered by police. His body has never been found.

The Malays' frustration grew when the Federation of Malaya became independent in 1957. Finding themselves marginalised, without no political leverage and only oppression and murder as the response to peaceful means, the irredentist Malay movement concluded that militancy was the only viable choice. In the 1960s, overt insurgency broke out. PULO (Patani United Liberation Organisation) and BRN (Barisan Revolusi Nasional) began waging guerrilla war against the Thai government along the southern border, coinciding with the emergence of communist insurgents in the northeast. As US military escalation in Vietnam fueled fears of a conflict nationwide, hundreds of millions of American dollars poured into infrastructure and security development to hold back the chaos in Thailand. In the 1980s, after a decade of failed counter-insurgency, General Prem's government resorted to a "persuasion over combat" strategy: support for Muslim cultural and religious rights, an economic development plan for the South and general amnesty for insurgents. After a relatively quiet period, corruption and poor policy implementation eroded public advocacy.

There was a recrudescence of conflict in 2004 as a consequence of the killing of 107 separatist militants in the Krue Se mosque in Pattani and, later that same year, the shooting of protesters by the authorities in Tak Bai district. The military rounded up 1,200 people and stacked them atop one another in trucks to be transported to an army camp. Nearly eighty of them died from suffocation and others were severely injured and lost their limbs. Since then, there has been a steady escalation of violence and every fresh outbreak adds to the deterioration of the area.

The political situation remains precarious. Attempts to establish peace talks have failed several times. The Thai administration blames the inability of the plethora of militant groups to reach common ground and stop the violence. But it is also true that the agenda behind those negotiations pursues a solution in terms of security rather than a genuine political will. The population is increasingly polarised and the Buddhist minority feels under siege. There has been a backlash by notorious Thai right-wing groups and ultra-nationalist firebrands. The bloodshed continues on an almost daily basis. A thick twist of intertwining strands including the internal politics of the army, corruption and drug trafficking contributes to it. The picture is unclear on every level. But one thing is certain. The bombings and shootings continue and there seems no end in sight to the conflict, and the people in other parts of the country do not seem to care.

The Thai government, particularly the junta, in place since the coup in 2014, is at pains to keep this conflict a domestic matter, as the shadow of ISIS reached several countries in Southeast Asia.

Every day there is news of the ongoing troubles in the South accompanied by pictures of suffering and destruction. Some of the images suggest an all-out war. I was not so foolhardy as to ignore these facts. The dangers are real enough and widespread in the entire region and the situation seemed unpredictable. Anything could happen anywhere, at any given moment of the day or night. But, at the same time, precisely because of the kind of coverage that this area had been receiving over the years, it had become alienated and set apart by an invisible frontier of fear. I took it as a challenge to cross this frontier with no preconceptions about what I would find there, guided by the compass of my intuition.

When I first visited Thailand's Deep South, I knew nothing about its history. I purposely refrained from researching the background of this troubled region demonised by the public, convinced that I should go there without bearing the weight of my own prejudgement, with no particular agenda except to drift around at leisure. My initial plan was to start my trip in Yala, as I had heard from a journalist that this provincial capital boasted a strong idiosyncrasy. From there, I would travel to Pattani and Narathiwat. Most of all, I wanted to allow myself the time and mindset to be exposed to what had to be discovered. What was clear to me was that I did not want to be there simply as another photojournalist trying to capture the drama in moments of violence or the trauma and pain in the aftermath of an armed encounter. I felt that such explicit images would not lead to a better understanding of the region. I was looking for something else – another dimension to the whole southern issue that might perhaps reveal aspects of the area that were not so blatantly trapped in the conflict. But I was far from clear as to what it was or whether I would be able to bring it to light.

Soon after arriving in Yala I bought a cheap bicycle. This was to be my main means of transport the whole time I was down south. I deliberately chose to use a bicycle believing, probably naively, that if I showed myself in a candid way, like an open target, I posed no threat to anyone and that the more conspicuous I was, the safer I would be. Besides, I learned there that public transport was more likely to be hit by roadside bombs. In any case, cycling around gave me a sense not just of joy and freedom, but also of connectedness with people. On a bicycle, I was offering my physical presence and inviting the response of those whose paths I crossed. And this turned out to be what happened. Everywhere I went people would look round and stare or do a double-take as I passed them by. It was always with a look of curiosity often accompanied by a smile. Sometimes, cars would stop and their drivers and passengers would flag me down to simply ask me if I needed anything. Some of them would hand me their phone numbers in case I needed help.

It was an eventful adventure. Muslims would invite me for lunch in their homes, while military personnel in plain clothes warned me against venturing upcountry. Welcomed to overnight in a mosque, while barred from setting foot in another; warned of the dangers in a village ahead, only to be warned again, upon getting there, of the hazards in the one from which I just came; a death threat that quickly morphed into gracious invitation at my arrival in a remote village; a night ride from Pattani to Yala, in which two teenagers on a scooter came alongside my bicycle, in what I feared would be a drive-by shooting, only for them to produce a mango, hand it to me and drive away without a word; a manager coached a soccer match, loudhailer in hand and assault rifle slung over his shoulder; Malays who joined militias fighting Malays; Buddhist temples made into army bases and leisure parks into military drill grounds. All these contradictions accompanied me throughout my journey.

I wandered aimlessly, always trying to see beyond the ongoing conflict, until I came across this mysterious house that seemed, somehow, more than just a building. This was a sanctuary of light and shadow, a poignant elegy to the solitude and memories carved in the region's divided soul, trapped in limbo, yearning for its forgotten splendour, held captive by its desolation.

The house urged me to look into the past. I would never have imagined that after crossing its entrance, and as the outside world closed behind me, it would draw me into the depths of my own consciousness.

What had begun as a photography project was eventually published in Bangkok as a photo book. It was the culmination of a four-year journey full of serendipity, a series of remarkable coincidences, such as my encounters with Tew Bunnag, to whom I owe gratitude for his advice as a writer and his introduction to Narisa Chakrabongse, the editor of my photo book. Both, as I would later find out, are strongly connected to the story I will relate, as their forefathers played a pivotal role in the region's destiny, akin to the struggle of my ancestors in medieval Spain. The House of Bunnag is an illustrious clan in Thailand, originated from a rich Persian merchant in the court of Ayutthaya. Among them were queens and consorts to the kings of Siam, and generals who led armies against the Burmese and the Vietnamese. As a matter of fact, Tew's great-grand uncle carried out the annexation of the seven Malay principalities and his great-great-grandfather was regent of King Chulalongkorn, who in turn, was great-great-grandfather of Narisa. My dear friend Hannan, who helped me delve into the house's past, is also linked to the house by family ties and through him, connections radiated out to others. In some strange way, the house has gathered us all.

We are what remains of our ancestors, carrying quiescent memories that may be invoked in unexpected ways by certain things, places or people for whom we feel a deep, yet inscrutable, affection, like the entreating message of nostalgia that assailed me the first time I set foot in the House of the Raja.

NOTE TO READER

The different spelling of "Patani" and "Pattani" in this book is deliberate. "Pattani" is the Thai spelling that refers to the province of present-day Thailand or its provincial city, while "Patani" is the Malay spelling for the name of the ancient Malay Kingdom.

Secrets of
Bang Nara

~ I ~

It all began with a chance invitation to tea. Sunlight had almost vanished, leaving Narathiwat with a bittersweet lethargy. The last call to prayer wafted through town, preluding silence. I found myself riding my bicycle through unlit, empty streets, gliding past weathered shophouses whose doors it seemed had never opened. As the world fell under the swathe of darkness, a feeling of serenity enfolded me. A few weeks earlier in Bangkok, I had heard of this far-off region: a neglected land, ravaged by bloody conflict and uncertainty; a land set apart by an invisible frontier of fear and foreboding, banished in a shadowy corner of public consciousness. I wanted to see that malign place for myself. Yet, now that I was here in the Deep South, this same land had not carved fear into my heart, but was enveloping me in a soothing blanket of obscurity.

"How strange it is to find peace within darkness," I was thinking when I saw them: two men who had improvised their own tea shop on the pavement, sitting under the dim light of a stucco porch. They drank their tea in quietude, as if the only inhabitants left in town, everyone else swallowed by the gloaming shadows. As I passed by, a rare westerner riding a bicycle, they eagerly beckoned me to join them. Soaked in sweat, craving a cooling bath in my hotel, I slowed hesitantly only to speed up again. Then, a final thought led me to pause.

It is impossible to find the extraordinary without opening ordinary doors.

I turned back and rode towards them, recognising the owner of a Chinese restaurant where I had breakfasted a few times. But it was the first time I had seen his companion, who greeted me in English, a man whose goatee and Middle Eastern features struck me as foreign but who, in fact, was a Thai-Muslim.

They inquired about me with all the usual questions I had been asked around the town, but dispensed with the local customary, "Aren't you scared to come here?" This time the looming army, the camps, road checkpoints, patrols, militias, helicopters and armoured vehicles were all dismissed by polite conversation over milky cups of *teh susu*.[1] The overwhelming military presence appeared so preposterous to me that I couldn't help but ask if it was really necessary. This sparked an argument between the two old friends.

The Muslim, Abdul Ghani, contended that the soldiers

---

1 Tea sweetened with condensed milk.

were unnecessary and that their presence actually exacerbated the conflict. His companion claimed that without them security would deteriorate rapidly because the army hampered insurgency. As our chat drew to a close, Abdul Ghani seemed to be itching to tell me something and finally when I stood up to leave, he made an announcement that would change the course of my journey across the Deep South: "Tomorrow, I will take you to the palace."

* * *

After a few nights at the Ocean Blue Mansion, a hotel whose only appeal was its name, I was keen to move on when I met a young northeastern Thai peddling his wares in the morning market. He laughed at my choice of accommodation, "You should come and see where I am staying. It's much nicer and cheaper!" he urged me. Although dubious, I followed the friendly man past rows of stalls to inspect his guesthouse, an inconspicuous building only a few minutes' walk away from the market. It turned out to be a pleasant surprise.

The Bang Nara Hotel had seen better days, its title taken from the former Narathiwat, renamed a century ago by King Rama VI. The provincial capital felt more like a small town than a city, nestled in the estuary of the Bang Nara River, whose waters meet those of the Gulf of Thailand and the South China Sea. With its teashops behind timber shopfronts, fishermen quarters and strands of beaches where lovers lolled in the shade of casuarina trees, Narathiwat had certainly changed but not at the brisk pace

XAVIER COMAS

of other parts of the country. Wooden houses with crumbling tile roofs stood their ground, fighting back an onslaught of modernity from the capital, surrounded by traffic, convenience stores and concrete office buildings, of which the most obtrusive was the Krung Thai Bank: a sleek, massive blue-glass cube that seemed to have flown all the way from Bangkok to crash-land right next to the Bang Nara Hotel. The two-storey building was easy to miss, concealed behind a beige timber façade in dire need of paint and the same discreet entrance you would find at any shophouse in town. But upon walking in, it was like stepping back in time to a Bang Nara of old. All in wood, its walls were assembled using slats like those of a ship's hull, everything but the flooring painted with a frolic of colours; a splash of aquamarine and turquoise on walls and ceilings, sky and peacock blue on window and door frames and a combination of chocolate with custard yellow on verandahs and stairways.

Most of the ground floor was a five-table eatery served by a kitchen just big enough to fit the two employees who functioned as cooks, waiters and receptionists. At the foot of the reception desk glowed a small red shrine devoted to some protective Chinese deity that you had to be careful not to trample when picking up your key. Past the restaurant and the staff quarters, a timber-decked walkway led through a backyard vegetable garden to some rooms at the end. Sitting on the floor in front of a balcony door, a few women enjoyed a midday meal. Behind them, a broad teak staircase with sturdy newels at the landings climbed to the upper floor, where I would be staying.

The stairs reached a homely hallway with a stout table in the centre and three rooms on each side. Behind the landing, on a terrace offering a hint of the street, two tiled bathrooms with squat toilets and showers were shared by guests. Gathering dust on a bamboo console table in the hallway was a 1980 edition of a travel guidebook, whose cover illustrated a globetrotter, his backpack shaped like the world.

At the end of the hallway, a double door opened onto one of the hotel's best features: a timber balcony with a criss-cross balustrade that spread across the river frontage, suspended on stilts above the water and freshened by the sea breeze off the gulf. From the balcony and across calm waters, a backdrop of white sand banks, gentle dunes and stands of palm trees unfurled. Beyond, a small mountain rose in the morning haze. No houses or construction betrayed the fact that this was downtown. With just the occasional sight of a fishing boat resting on the shore or the white speck of a distant goat grazing, the view created the illusion of being adrift on the river in a vintage sailing ship.

My room was humble but cosy, suffused every morning with different hues when sunrays washed through stained glass windows that looked out on the river. The furniture was all made of wood and painted in the same shades of greens and blues: a rustic bed that filled nearly a third of the space, a mirror cabinet, a clothes-drying rack, a coffee table with two chunky chairs and a ceiling fan that swung back and forth threatening to tumble.

The hotel manager, a Thai-Chinese man in his seventies with a bunch of amulets dangling from his neck and who appeared from time to time to move with difficulty, did not know when the building was built but assured me that it was more than 100 years old. After the Second World War, the property was transferred to a Pashtun businessman from present-day Pakistan who rented rooms upstairs to textile traders and spaces downstairs to several well-known restaurants. Eventually, it was renovated and the establishment reopened its doors exclusively as a budget hotel.

I woke with the dawn. Lying in bed, my eyes alighted first on the green of the ceiling. Reflections from the river's surface quivered anxiously around the fan like a soul trapped on its way to the other world. For a moment, the image was an extension of my dreams, sweeping away into the whirlwind. As the sun ascended and the room steadily warmed, the reflections slowly faded until the spectral vision evaporated before my eyes.

Outside in the hallway, scarlet light gilded the turquoise walls. Fishing boats trailed the blood-red waters of the Bang Nara River out to the South China Sea. Their rumble seemed not to bother a quiet gecko clinging to the window in the corner. I wondered if he was dead, but when I tried to touch him, he stirred nervously for a second.

I had a shower, put on fresh clothes and headed downstairs. On my way out, I came across an incredibly thin old man plodding along the walkway. As wizened as tree bark, his bony limbs poked out of his t-shirt and shorts like twigs. Dragging his flip-flops in short, weary steps, the energy in his body seemed about to drain away. "Here is the laundry man!" I heard a woman announce.

On the street, motorbikes, pick-ups and rickshaws roared past carrying fruits, food carts, birdcages and high school students. I crossed over to the market for breakfast. Rows of motorbikes were parked with their saddles fully open – one of the security measures enforced to prevent bombs from being planted inside. Heavily armed young soldiers and militiamen kept their positions flanking the market gate, sitting on benches in the back of trucks or entrenched behind a pile of durians, eyes vigilant, fingering their weapons. I paused by the gate, to give way to a line of monks in saffron robes that ambled into the enclosure. They were accompanied by watchful youths in plain clothes carrying silk satchels which concealed guns, according to the locals.

The market was heaving, segregated into the Buddhist section to the south and the three-times-larger Muslim section to the north. The spread of colourful delicacies kept me looking around before making my choices, exchanging smiles with a gaggle of noisy vendors, many of whom seemed amused, while a few others looked perplexed at the only Westerner around. Reaching the Buddhist-Muslim fringes, the smell from the chicken and fish combined into a biting stench.

I paused to stare at a blood-soaked pile of catfish heads; behind, a man took fish from a plastic crate, slashed their heads off, chopped the bodies into slices and threw them in black rubbish bags. Inside the crate, two or three fish squirmed in a desperate struggle to escape the soggy mass of death below. Then a woman hauled out a metre-long live catfish and threw it with a thud onto the concrete floor, where it thrashed violently. Even after two blows to the head with an iron bar the fish was still writhing. The man behind her stopped slashing heads, jumped up, seized the bar from her and in a near-frenzy clubbed the catfish's head again and again until it didn't move. The scene transfixed me until someone carrying goods on a rickshaw brought me back to the present and I moved aside.

On my way out, shirtless Muslim men chopped carcasses and tore the flesh from hanging cow legs before a wall smeared with dried blood. Axes in hand, amid viscera and tissue, these men were the friendliest in the market. They greeted me eagerly, asked where I was from and howled with laughter at my answer – Barcelona – all the while smashing bones and crushing skulls, blasting bits and pieces every which way, prompting me to duck.

Later that morning, Abdul fetched me from the hotel with his friend Azman, a tall and immaculate university lecturer who greeted me in polite English with a keen, broad smile. Azman drove us along a river promenade with plazas, formal gardens and a Royal pavilion in Manila style. The road diverted for a moment from the watercourse, passed a park delimited by century-old rubber trees and rejoined the river at a humble neighbourhood on the outskirts of town. Soon we passed a small mosque with glistening green domes, and turned left onto a narrow dirt track. As we slowly made our way, I was assailed by an obnoxious odour, unfamiliar to me. It came from a nearby rubber warehouse, they explained. We continued until the trail opened onto common land that bordered the riverbank. Azman stopped the car. Before us, amid soaring coconut palms and mature jackfruit trees, sprawled an ancient wooden mansion.

Visibly dilapidated, the rambling structure rested on numerous stilts supported by massive stuccoed bases and crowned with a double-tiered roof made of terracotta tiles that from a distance looked like dragon scales. Eaves overhung with a fretwork of spiky fronds running along their edges like rows of broken fangs. Woodcarvings embellished walls and, on top, ridge crests in the shape of spears stood defiant, thrusting skyward. The apex of the central front gable was surmounted by a sculptured finial in the form of leaves that curled upwards. I could make out the outline of a lotus bud engraved on it. From the left wing, only a skeleton of rotten beams remained and parts of the roof and walls had been repaired in a haphazard way with plywood and corrugated zinc sheets that were already crumbling. In the very centre of the building, a steep staircase climbed to a verandah.

We ascended the steps and paused in front of an arched entrance with a wooden double door over which was large calligraphy in white chalk. Using my fairly basic language skills, I tried to decipher what I thought were Thai characters, only to be told by Abdul that it was actually Arabic writing proclaiming, "Allah".

* * *

We remove our shoes and as we enter an airy foyer, two women in veils and sarongs emerge from the shadows at the back to greet us, as though we are expected. Behind them three boys and a little girl, all holding back, seem afraid of me. I cannot be sure if I am welcome but after greeting the women with a smile, they respond with warmth.

"You can take pictures," Abdul tells me after a brief exchange with the women in Malay. "But be careful where you step, the flooring might collapse," he adds. I take this as permission for me to wander around at will, heeding his warning about the floor.

Sure enough, the floorboards creak under my bare feet, many of them weakened by rain, while others are rotted or missing, leaving scattered gaps. On the right side of the foyer are two doors. One is fastened with a padlock, while through the other, half-closed, I make out an empty room decorated with woodcarving panels on windows and a floor that looks too damaged to walk on. Towards the rear, the foyer opens to the exterior, flanked by loose balustrades that have been hurriedly secured with scraps of metal wire.

I walk with care across the uneven floor, while Azman explains, "We call this place *Rumoh Rajo*, which means the 'House of the Raja' in Malay." I nod at the sobriquet, but as I look at the broken architecture, with few signs of its former opulence, I can't help but wonder how this could have been the residence of a ruler. I ask them to tell me more about the house's history and who lived there, but neither Azman nor Abdul is able to offer further information.

I enter a spacious, almost empty hall with large doors on every side. Here two objects draw my attention. In the penumbra of a corner hangs a large kite with a half-moon shape made of bamboo stems and glazed paper painted with flowery patterns. Attached to it is a bow with rattan string that I am told plays a melody when the kite flies. Confined to silence, it seems to beg to sing with the wind again. In the opposite corner, partially draped with a batik cloth, stands a tall Victorian safe eaten by rust with a combination lock. I wonder what is inside.

Most of all, I am in awe of the light and shadows that fill the old building. Strands of light sneak in through cracks and fissures in the walls, floor and ceiling; fat beams and delicate filigrees in which dust particles gently dance, while a far corner is bathed in thick, velvety darkness. If not for this light, the interior would be ashen and sombre like a mausoleum, but, as it is, I get a sensation of suspended fragility as if I am in a foundering ship. The finery that once covered the skeleton I am walking through has long vanished, yet, in a way I cannot understand, I feel that something else has remained.

I move towards the back and enter another hall with more rooms and two stairways. At the rear, two double doors as tall as the ceiling open into a courtyard. I venture out. A few brick steps descend to a space surrounded by stucco walls scarred by rain and encrusted with patches of moss and lichen, ferns creeping out of cracks and crevices. Near the courtyard's centre is a serviceable round well, with a tin bucket attached to a rope alongside. On the right wall, behind a bulky wood door falling into pieces with rot, I notice the outline of a gate rendered impassable by a tree that has sprouted up right in front of it. Further back, two square bath pools fade behind a tangle of weeds, among scattered pieces of old furniture, shards of glass and bric-a-brac. Half of the ground is overgrown with shrubs and untended banana trees left to flourish as they please. Debris abounds. Abdul, apparently sensing my disappointment, motions with his hand and guides me back inside, saying, "Let's go upstairs. It's very beautiful there."

Unsure of what to expect, I climb one of the staircases. It opens out to a large, desolate attic under a pitched ceiling about seven metres high with multiple cross gables supported by an intricate truss of ironwood beams and columns. Sunlight flows in through carvings on floor-level windows and between gables, sieved by the foliage of surrounding trees, bathing the space with gentle shades of green and yellow, and a faint fragrance of what I can only fathom as incense pervades the air. Here, the atmosphere falls deeper under a shroud of solitude.

I find myself taken aback by an emptiness laden with a gravid silence, a silence with the anticipatory quality of a pause just before something is whispered. As I take heed of this, I feel a pull from deep within this strange building; for there is a lingering sense of painful separation, of something being abandoned in a hurry, of unfinished affairs and grief. I am carried away by the riddle and when it is time for us to bid our farewells, I know without a doubt that I will return.

* * *

On our way back, I buried myself in thought. "Go on, take as many pictures as you like," Abdul and Azman had told me several times during the half hour we spent walking around the building. They must have been puzzled because I took none. How could I explain – since I was as yet unclear about it myself – that from the moment I set foot in the house I was so struck by its timeless aura, mesmerised by the dignified solitude that filled the place, and, at the same time, startled by my feelings of affinity with it, that taking even a single shot felt trivial.

In fact, I could not get the house out of my mind. When heading back there on my own that very afternoon, I wondered whether the women would welcome me again. I parked my bicycle among the forest of pillars under the building, startling a cock perched on a pile of discarded beams, climbed the stairs and paused on the verandah to look at the Arabic characters I had earlier mistaken for Thai script. A few pairs of sandals lay scattered at my feet. The doorway was half-open, but I could not catch sight of anyone inside.

"Hello?" I called into the void. There was no reply. I looked in to see that the double door at the back of the foyer was closed, preventing me from seeing further and allowing me only to see some dishes and teacups left on the floor. The door creaked as I pushed it and tentatively took a step inside. A lattice of light and shadow received me. A ginger cat lay curled asleep on an old mattress trashed in a corner. "Hello?" I called again, this time louder, waking the cat. He squinted at me with his amber eyes only to close them again. Then, the door at the end opened and the women whom I had met earlier came forth, swaddled in sarongs. They showed no surprise on seeing me, but simply smiled.

I was welcomed in and shown to a bamboo bench in the foyer, where they invited me to sit. Then, one of them brought me hot tea. The women did not ask me anything right away and instead watched smiling in silence as I sipped the tea. I then felt drowsy, perhaps caused by the heat or the soothing atmosphere. Noticing what was happening, the women gestured assent and withdrew to let me rest. In a moment, I fell asleep.

When I awoke, there was a tray with a plate of fruit and a fresh cup of tea beside me, but no sign of the women and children. Even the ginger cat had disappeared. I sat, had a slice of pineapple and finished the tea. Afterwards, unsure of what to do, I scanned my surroundings. A weakening sunlight mellowed the shadows, impregnating the interior of the building with a balmy calmness. Outside, under a satiny blue vault, lofty coconut trees sagged, peeking in at me. I rose to my feet and ambled into the back of the house reaching the last hall, where the two women sat leisurely on a rattan mat with their children. They asked me if I had had a good rest and gestured to me to join them. I nodded, sat down and, with my Thai and an eagerness to communicate on both sides, we made ourselves understood fairly well.

The women were sisters. They were from a remote jungle village close to the border with Malaysia in a rugged district called Sisakorn. I had not travelled that far south yet, but had heard that behind those mountains, in the depths of Hala Bala forest, hid an elusive tribe and that the roads in the area were under the sway of the insurgency.

Fatimah was the youngest of the sisters. In her early thirties, she was still pretty, with smooth features on a round face that gave her a frail innocence, although in her eyes that naivety was tinged with sadness, as if something had been long ago broken inside her. Her husband was often away working for days at a time, with few hours devoted to his sons, Irfan and Montri, 12 and 8 years old, respectively. Time had been less forgiving with her older sister, Faridah. Married twice, with two children from different fathers and separated from her last husband, she exuded the sort of strength carved by the endurance of hardship. She had an angular face, prominent cheekbones and obsidian eyes that glinted in dim light, but she was reassuring and warm. Her laugh showed a few missing teeth, a painful memento from her last marriage, I learned later. She was very fond of her six-year-old daughter, Waesuraini, while there seemed to be a more distant relationship with her 12-year-old son, Pantawong. What intrigued me about Faridah was a flair for guessing whatever I struggled to say. It was not so much that she could tell what words I was trying to say in Thai – I often had to look them up in my dictionary before carrying on the conversation – but rather that she *knew* what I had in my mind to say.

During our chat, nothing was revealed as to why they had moved to this house, whether they were the homeowners or just landladies, but I was in no hurry to know the answer. The moment they asked me why I was interested in Narathiwat and what I was looking for there, I realised how difficult it was to respond with clarity. Since my arrival in the neighbouring city of Yala just before New Year's Eve, I had been wandering around the Deep South on a bicycle I had bought there, trying to see with my camera beyond the veil of conflict. As a photographer, I wanted to discover what lay behind the tragic picture of a place feared and loathed by people, but after weeks in remote villages and towns, none of the images I had taken felt special and nothing had urged me to stay until I arrived at this house. Certainly, now that I was here, the notion that chance had taken me to something pregnant with secrets awaiting to be unearthed was taking hold, but there was a reason for me to travel to the Deep South in the first place: an urge to plunge into the unknown, the mysterious. I could not conceive of life without it. Trying to understand what was behind this impulse of mine to divert from what would be considered the blessings of a normal life was something I struggled to comprehend since my childhood. Only after leaving behind a life that wanted me settled to travel alone could I untangle the incongruous way I felt about the world, the cognisance that fleeting moments of sheer happiness were also those aroused by uncertainty, far from friends and family.

My father told me once to imagine life as a measureless façade with an infinite number of doors. Most people are content to confine themselves to opening the few within their reach, while some strive to open as many as they can, hankering to see what lies on the other side. Making decisions is the most difficult thing in life, he said, because it is upon which doors you decide to open that sets the course of our pathways. His words resound now stronger than ever, wondering if we are the ones who choose those doors or if they actually open before us, like the one opened by the hand of serendipity onto this house. Sharing these thoughts with the sisters was beyond my language skills, but I spared no effort to explain myself and even tried to find the word "serendipity" in my English-Thai dictionary, to no avail. But Faridah did not need words. She understood.

The sisters granted me permission to explore the building freely. Driven by an innocent curiosity, the children dogged my steps as I made my way around. If I stopped and turned back, they would scamper away to hide. Every now and then I played with them, although they were still too shy to talk. Their giggles and teasing mingled with the emptiness and decay through which we wandered, filling me with a mixture of happiness and melancholy, as if our games were a re-enactment of the merrymaking of former times in this once grand mansion.

From that day on, I paid regular visits to the house, often stopping by the stalls across from the nearby mosque to buy local sweets for the children and some food or drinks for their mothers. I felt that Fatimah and Faridah truly appreciated my company and my concern.

* * *

Soon I understood the presence of the women downstairs at the Bang Nara Hotel. My 'sailing ship' was actually a brothel. Whenever locals asked me where I was staying, the mention of this unsavoury place would spark either hoots of laughter or cringes. For me, the seedy reputation of the hotel only added to its already charming eccentricity.

Even the old manager, a native of Narathiwat himself,

couldn't tell me when the hotel had undergone its inglorious transformation. From what he could remember, prostitutes already dwelled in it when he was a boy. They occupied all the rooms except for the six on the upper floor of the rear wing, reserved exclusively for ordinary guests.

The women of the Bang Nara, although sometimes rowdy, were mostly good-natured and helpful. From the north and northeast of the country, they came to ply their trade with that growing sense of resignation at approaching middle-age, their sons and daughters left behind. The distant and feared Deep South kept their occupation from their relatives and friends, who believed them to be working in Bangkok as masseurs or roving street vendors. Contrary to my first impression, the women did not work for the hotel but were self-employed. They checked in to lodge for months, if not years, and paid the daily rate of 150 baht just like any other guest, allowing them to carry out their business without interference. Then, with enough savings, they would return to their villages for a while to give a hand during rice harvest season or to spend time with their families. They kept in touch with other women in hotels of this sort across the south so that when one of them moved out, she would send word for a fellow worker to fill in.

Customers took the liberty to turn up at any time, even early in the morning, when the women were still putting on make-up, grooming themselves or having their breakfast. Quiet men stood about idly, watching whatever the ladies busied themselves with and hoping for them to be available. Even when she had finished, a woman might still reject a customer, depending on her mood or whether she liked him. Business could get pretty hectic at the end of the month right after payday, cash filling the pockets of soldiers and locals or even some insurgent in disguise who queued in front of the love rooms, waiting patiently his turn. The regular fee was 300 baht for a 20-minute session, a price that to some appeared excessive. "In Tanjong Mas[2] it costs only 150 baht!" a customer complained to me once.

The women rarely left the premises except to shop at the market across the street. Having much time to spare, they liked to garden, exercise, idle on their beds watching TV, play cards or even catch fish from the balcony, and above all, they devoted themselves to cooking, preparing impossible amounts of spicy food that flavoured the hallway's ambience with the aroma of fish sauce, garlic and curry paste. Friendly and easy-going, they often invited me to share a meal, always a good occasion for them to have a laugh whenever the burn of chili twisted my face and for me to learn a little about them.

Om was the only one from Bangkok, where she used to work in a beauty salon. Her husband had been shot dead by a street gang, and shortly after she gave birth to a baby girl, her only child. Her daughter was now married, with kids and lived in the capital. Asking if she missed her, the bitter tone in her response preceded her words.

"Not at all. Things got rough between us. She only contacts

---

2 Tanjong Mas is a subdistrict of Rangae, one of the "Red Zone" districts in Narathiwat province under the influence of militants.

me when she's running out of money, but I am always happy to help. After all, she is my daughter."

She decided to take a traditional massage course and secured employment at spas for a while until a friend working as a hostess in a karaoke parlour encouraged her to move on to this more lucrative job.

"It was fun, but once you start making easy money, you soon want more. My friend and I came to the south to work as freelancers in hotels. We went to Hat Yai, Patalung, Yala. I like it more here, it's quiet and peaceful, even if people think it's dangerous. Some girls get nice stuff, a fridge, a big TV, then they are reluctant to move. But I get bored and keep moving. I am going to Pattani next."

Om did not shy away from speaking with the utmost frankness about her job. "Here things get a bit more relaxed. I like Muslim clients because they don't grope in excess or try to kiss my lips or lick my breast. It's quicker to get it done because they are the easiest to turn on. It must be because they don't drink alcohol, although some of them take drugs. There are men who come just to talk about their personal problems and family issues. I give them 10 extra minutes for the same price."

These women, with their openness and forbearance, embracing the twists and turns of life, grew on me. I had a problem with only one, who, despite being the youngest and shortest, possessed the most forceful character, well suited for her side job as a zealous housekeeper. She never grew tired of warning me constantly to respect the curfew that started at nine, a particularly irksome rule with which I could not help but often fail to comply. This inconvenient crackdown was not enforced in other establishments but I had grown so fond of the place that I decided to stay.

Life in the Bang Nara was free and easy but never monotonous. A woman engrossed herself knitting a fishing net oblivious to the soldier next to her trying to haggle over the service fee, while another stood on the walkway, wiggling her hips with a pink hula hoop to fight obesity, an epidemic that seemingly had afflicted the hotel's population. One of them sneaked upstairs to dry fish on the balcony, safe from the reach of cats; not for her own consumption, but, as she explained to me with great joy, to post to her family in Chiang Mai. Probably one of the most outlandish sights was a creature that one early morning swam beneath the balcony. No one believed I had seen a crocodile.

The upper floor, where Chinese gold traders, Thai vendors and the unlikely traveller spent the night, had also become a frugal haven for the occasional retired expatriate and Western derelict, who had chosen not to finish their lonely days in the cold of their native lands, but in the sultry debauchery of the Bang Nara.

Over the course of the weeks, two other foreigners checked in. One of them was an Asian man who spent his time sitting quietly alone. I only dared to address him once, introducing myself and asking where he was from, hoping for a conversation. But the only word the man spared with me was "Tokyo". Then he lapped into silence, his eyes fixed somewhere ahead and he would just stay like that, so that he became almost invisible, until one day he vanished all together, never to be seen again.

The second foreigner I met was a short and pale Chinese-Malaysian man in his late sixties who seemed never to leave the Bang Nara. He told me that he would stay for a month and that this had been his holiday, once a year, for the past 40 years. His walk, waddling around wrapped in a bath sarong, reminded me of a penguin. Asking him if Narathiwat had changed much since his first visit, he reckoned, "Yes, for the better", without further elaboration on how military occupation could mean improvement.

The only permanent foreign resident in the hotel turned out to be my next-door neighbour, a friendly retired Parisian of Vietnamese origin, who had been occupying a room for two years. His family back in France had stopped talking to him but he seemed to accept it. Everyone called him Peter, which did not sound French at all; he had been so christened by one of the girls because his original name, René, Thais found unpronounceable. He didn't go out too often and, when he did, never returned later than five in the evening because glaucoma had substantially diminished his night vision. Always eager to share his useful tips for getting around town, we soon became good friends. He was the only tinge of European dissent in the hotel, with his "Stupid soldiers! There is nothing going on here!" and nostalgic evenings with Ella Fitzgerald emanating from his room across the landing.

Peter spent his days making the rounds to the ladies' rooms and the evenings getting drunk on beer accompanied by his last conquest. Occasionally, a retired Dutch gentleman with a haggard face joined him. He lived in Kelantan, but crossed the border to use the hotel as a rendezvous for illicit encounters with young local men, most of them married with children. He addressed me in Spanish, one of the nine languages he spoke fluently, wheezing, pausing at times to catch his breath. Eventually he stopped coming and we learned that he had passed away alone in his home. Friendship between retirees was short-lived in this part of the world.

In truth, there was little to do in the late-night hours, moments I took to withdraw in solitude. Reclined on the balcony under a shimmering canopy, I would gaze into the coal-black void that stretched before me and let my thoughts take wing and fly with the breeze over the river. Sometimes, a narrow beam of light bobbed from a small fishing boat that passed silently below, scouring the dark waters for the night's catch. In those moments nothing else existed, the faint cackle of the women gambling with clients on the ground floor the only whiff of reality.

* * *

My regular visits to the house, often stretched into dusk, naturally did not go unnoticed by the neighbours. At first I am sure that they viewed me with suspicion, but once they were used to my comings and goings they began to greet me with smiles and, little by little, I even became acquainted with several of them: the old Thai-Chinese couple at the wooden shophouse where the sisters bought their groceries; the elderly men who liked to sit in front of the mosque after prayers watching passers-by; the crowds who hung out at the nearby tea shops; the families at the roadside food stalls purveying their home-cooked desserts (I became really addicted to their coconut pudding wrapped in banana leaf); the workers at the rubber warehouse; the clique of youths indulging in betting on fish-fighting and the Muslim Muay Thai teacher living next to the house who helped a group of children to overcome their drug addiction. They were all friendly to me and seemed to share the same curiosity: why is this foreigner on a bicycle not afraid to come here?

I learned from elders that this neighbourhood was called Kampung Takok, which in vernacular Malay means "Village of Fear". According to them, this had long ago been an area that could only be accessed by boat, sandwiched between thick jungle and riverbanks frequented by wild elephants, tigers and crocodiles that congregated to bask atop a red boulder in the middle of the river. With the menace of the natural world long gone, the neighbourhood's inauspicious name was now embodied in the gloomy Rumoh Rajo. People seemed to know nothing or little else about the enigmatic building other than tales of hauntings and apparitions. Many were convinced that sinister forces inhabited it. My casual attempts to get a piece of information out of the locals would always fail, the usual answers being "Oh, that is a very old house" or "It's been there for a long time".

Adding to the local lore was the neighbours' aversion to the sisters. While Fatimah could count on the support of her husband, it was unclear how Faridah and her kids subsisted. The sisters always stayed in, or, at least, I never saw them venturing outside during my visits, while the children always idled indoors or played around, never off at school. I didn't dare to ask them about it. On the whole, it meant that the family rarely left the compound. I am not sure if voluntarily or for some reason I ignored, but they hedged themselves in the suspended space and tempo of the house. Their seclusion led to gossip from women in the community who regarded them as layabouts, dubious outsiders with no right to stay in such a grand place – prejudices that might have more to do with fear and jealousy. I began to think of how fortunate or even privileged I was for being able to travel at will between two overlapping, yet estranged realities, the world in which we all live and another one that only existed within the confines of those wooden walls.

Every other week I would run into Fatimah's husband, a short, thin, middle-aged man whose name I constantly forgot. His appearances clashed with the old-world air of the house; pink long-sleeved shirt, wrinkle-free white flannel pants, milky leather shoes and oversized gangsta sunglasses. He earned his living as an itinerant singer at village weddings, festivals and local fairs in the region and that is how he had met and courted Fatimah when she was an ingenuous teenager. Impressed by show business, she married him at the age of 18. Only after the birth of her second son did Fatimah find out that the prolonged absences of her husband under the pretext of work concealed a secret. He had another family; in fact, from long before Fatimah took his hand. His first wife and four other children lived in Yingo, a small town 12 kilometres from Narathiwat. His secret uncovered, he resorted to allotting alternate weeks to each of his wives to keep them satisfied. Fatimah, finding herself without the financial resources to divorce and concerned for the well-being of her children, resigned herself to accept his new terms and endure her status as the second spouse. To make matters worse, the older first wife not only rejected Fatimah but also regarded her with disdain.

Fatimah's husband did not display any overt reaction to my presence, but I could tell that my keen interest and the frequency of my visits disconcerted him. When meeting me, he hid behind a rehearsed aura of self-assurance and authority that kept both of us apart. During the time he spent in the house, I never saw him being affectionate towards his children. Little Irfan would try to gain his attention by cuddling on his lap, but his father preferred to devote most of his sporadic stays to his second wife behind closed doors or ensconced in his divan smoking in silence, his bland gaze lost at the ceiling. Fatimah cheered up with his company only to shrivel again when he left. "I have been unfortunate," she would complain, lying down listlessly and staring into space, convinced she was under the influence of sorcery concocted by the resentful first wife. Such a vicious curse could only be the doing of a necromancer, using oil extracted from the chin of a pregnant woman's corpse who had met a violent death. The spell would have been carried out around an embryonic effigy immersed in that consecrated oil and brought to a cemetery to invoke the ghost of a stillborn upon her.

Before long, I realised there were others staying in the house. Two or three young men in their early twenties occupied the room I had seen in the right wing whose door was under lock and key. They entered their room using a makeshift ladder under the building and through a trap door. I was told that they were allowed to stay in return for doing various odd jobs – repairing, cleaning and helping with the electricity bills from time to time. They did not seem to mind my presence. Although I hardly saw them, let alone have the opportunity to talk to them, if ever our paths crossed they greeted me with a brief smile of recognition. I did not give them much thought until a few months later...when the soldiers came.

* * *

When I explored around Narathiwat my main landmark was an imposing red brick clock-tower decorated with arabesque stained glass that stood in the centre of a roundabout which I passed many times a day. To the north lay the morning market, Narathat beach and the fishermen's quarters with its exotic *kolek* boats, to the east the Bang Nara River with the Bang Nara Hotel on its banks, to the south the House of the Raja, and to the west the Buddhist and Chinese temples where worshippers lent their bodies to the gods and walked on fire. In every direction, the town was an experience, where one just needed to wander around for things to happen. As often as not, I encountered the dark and lonely figures of demented men wrapped in their scruffy sarongs shambling barefoot around the town or standing motionless as wraiths in the shadows. At other times, I would stumble across someone so out of place it was as if he had been teleported from a faraway country to this no-man's-land. An African man on a toy-like pink bicycle, bedecked in a garish purple suit and pink tie, matching handkerchief jutting from his breast pocket, and spotless white leather shoes, peddled around under the blazing sun as if trying to find his way home. One evening, a man popped up in the middle of a deserted beach at nightfall, dressed in a fluorescent yellow biking outfit, a golf club in his hands, stretching his arms about to hit the ball on the sand towards the twilight sky.

Striking up a conversation with almost anyone was effortless, particularly in the laid-back tea shops, omnipresent shelters from the midday heat where I became acquainted with a medley of characters: a long-bearded Imam with a stern look who invited me to share a meal with *dawah*[3] students at his mosque; a senator escorted by several bodyguards who treated me to tea and curry puffs while his handgun lay openly on the table; or a school director who offered me a job teaching English – it was not easy to find foreigners willing to work in a region where insurgents torched schools and killed teachers and headmasters, presumably seen as instruments of the Thai state to assimilate the Malays.

The friendliness of the locals made it hard to believe that this was considered one of the most dangerous places in Southeast Asia. Instead of bullets or bombs, I met frankness and spontaneity. More than once I asked for the bill in a restaurant, only to be told that another customer had already paid for me before leaving. No

---

3 *Dawah* usually denotes missionary work for Islam. Mosques and other Islamic centers sometimes spread dawah actively, similar to evangelical churches.

sooner had I walked into an adorned cul-de-sac where a Malay wedding party was in progress than I was pulled in to join the feast and become a fanciful prop in the visual memories of the couple's happiest day. The hospitality always went furthest with the Muslims who often invited me to their homes and introduced me to their families with food, beverages and lively conversation.

Locals were so friendly that their attention could sometimes be overwhelming. When the urge to get away from everything arose, I would flee to Ao Manao (Lime Bay), six kilometres south of the house. The bay was at the end of a long white beach that stretched southwards from the Bang Nara River estuary. It encompassed a fishing village nestled along mangroves, open pastures interspersed by marshy lagoons and evergreen pine forest that shed a blanket of leaves abut the road. Here, cows, goats and cats lived together in harmony, loafing on the beach, whilst the occasional lone fisherman waded along the foreshore, shifting the sand with his hands in search of scallops. The southernmost tip of the bay ended in a beautiful cove marked by Bukit Tanjong, the same mountain seen from the balcony of the Bang Nara Hotel, and where rainforest sheltered the Thaksin Ratchaniwet Royal Palace. According to local elders, hidden in that forest was a cave inhabited in the past by a hermit under whose instruction shamans trained in the craft of magical arts. I tried to find it once, but I could not proceed deep enough because a military wire fence restricted the pass.

A trail skirted the mountain and meandered gently down under the shade of horsetail casuarinas to the seashore. From there, an easy scramble over large granite boulders led to a few secluded sandy coves. Deserted of man, this was the only place where I could be truly alone, and over time, became a private retreat from my own thoughts, in moments of unease.

* * *

As the days passed, my visits to the family became routine and I began to be more involved in their daily lives, sharing meals and bathing from the well in the courtyard. They lent me a sarong to wear for those blissful rituals that, in no time, I came to relish.

The children had gradually become accustomed to my being around and, owing to my affection for them, started to see me less as a *farang*[4] and more as a friend they could trust. In the absence of their fathers, I felt that my male presence comforted them and as time went by, Faridah and Fatimah saw me as a fraternal figure for their children.

My wanderings around the south had come to a halt. Part of me saw this as an interruption in my adventure. I began mulling over possible itineraries and even set a date on the calendar, vowing to myself that when that day came, I would leave behind Narathiwat. But that day would never arrive. The thought of parting became unbearable, and whenever I tried to overcome it, I would find myself making up excuses to postpone my departure time and time again. The strength to tear myself away from the house and the family gradually waned until I reduced my travel

4 A generic Thai word for someone Caucasian.

plans to cycling day trips within the province.

"What is holding me here?" I asked myself. Was it my empathy for this old house or my affection for the family? Perhaps both. The family and the house embodied the same quality of loneliness and obscurity, the idea of something so detached from its surrounding reality that it had created its own. Why I felt drawn to such a world of desolation remained as yet unanswered. All I knew was that every time I set foot in the House of the Raja, it felt like entering into a privy sanctuary of peace that embraced me.

Several weeks later, my affection for this family had grown to such an extent that I was bewildered by the strength with which recollections of particular shared moments had rooted deep inside me: Fatimah tenderly trimming her son's hair in the warmth of the morning light; little Waesuraini closing her eyes while her mother powdered her face after a bath; the shadow play of figures cast by the children's hands on patches of light that spattered across the attic. All these scenes came to me under prickling stars as I stood alone on the balcony of the Bang Nara before an expanse of darkness. Then, all at once, an inexplicable sorrow would overcome me as if those memories belonged to a world that had already ceased to exist, both the family and the house a figment of my mind.

* * *

My afternoons at the house were occupied with sporadic English lessons for the sisters and playtime with the children. One evening, the lessons went on longer than usual. Even pedalling at the fastest pace I would not be able to reach the hotel before it shut its doors. I would have to deal with the housekeeper's irritability once more. Seeing my reluctance to leave, the sisters suggested that I stay overnight since there were many empty rooms. I had just agreed when Abdul Ghani, the man who had brought me to the house, telephoned me asking me to join him and his friend Azman for tea. When I declined politely, explaining that I was in the Rumoh Rajo and had been invited to stay, he responded with alarm, "No, no. That's impossible. I'm coming to pick you up in 10 minutes. We can talk later!"

Abdul drove me to a market near Narathat beach, where an outdoor cinema had been improvised under a pavilion. The place was crowded. Some attendees kept their attention fixed on the screen where a Chinese drama was being projected, while others chose to chat. Azman sat alone by a table at the back. He welcomed me with his broad, perpetual smile.

"Please, sit down. Would you like to have tea or roti[5]?" he asked, offering me a seat between him and Abdul.

"Both please. I didn't know you had a cinema here," I said, pleasantly surprised.

"Of course we do. Do you see? We also have a life here, you know. Look around you, all is normal. Please tell your friends in Bangkok about it," he responded.

---

5 A Southeast Asian version of the pan-fried flatbread from India, made most often from wheat flour and egg and often served with curries as a snack accompanied by tea or coffee.

It was cool season but that night had grown hot and humid. Three cups of *teh susu* with ice and a plate of egg roti arrived at the table. We cooled off with the tea, sweet and tasty. Azman picked a slice of roti dripping with condensed milk and, before putting it into his mouth, gave me a sidelong glance asking, "You've been going to the palace on your own, haven't you?"

Clearly, Abdul had told him of my intention to spend the night there as the conversation moved abruptly to a lecture.

"You must never stay in a Muslim home with women if a male relative is not around. That is our culture. To do so would be dangerous for them as well as for you. Think of what the neighbours could think or do," said Azman, his smile intact.

"I am just their friend, nothing else," I objected.

"It doesn't matter. I know you are a good man, but other people don't know you." At this Abdul nodded in agreement.

I could not bring myself to reply, but only smile and nod. At first, it felt unfair to be rebuked in this way, like being treated as a naughty boy. I had found his words offensive because they questioned my probity. But the truth was that this was my first time among Muslims and I knew little about their social customs. No matter how well intentioned, a single white man living under the same roof with Muslim women whose husbands were absent would, without doubt, stir up all sorts of rumours. It behoved me to respect the concerns of someone to whom I owed the discovery of the house.

Seeing me downcast and silent, Azman ended on a conciliatory note, saying, "You should embrace Islam. My religion is one of convenience. It teaches you how to behave, how to dress, even how to eat!"

* * *

One evening, a man I had never seen before came to the house. As he was about to leave, we crossed paths by the doorway. He was clad in traditional Malay fashion in a plaid sarong, batik shirt and white *kopiah*, a Muslim skullcap. He had a swarthy visage, his age hard to determine, and exuded an aura that was both ancient and obscure. Upon seeing me, the man did not utter a word, but paused and turned back to train a veiled gaze on me. His dark, fat lips under a black moustache pulled into a grin, showing off his denture. He then walked down the stairs and out of the house to merge with the moonless night.

Later that week, while teaching English to Faridah and Fatimah, I had the odd sensation that someone was watching us. I turned around to see that there, under the threshold of the door, stood a dark figure. The scant light sketched his face, but from his silhouette I could guess that this was the same man. How long he had been there, I couldn't tell. The figure drew closer and spoke in broken Thai "Last night, I was here looking at you. I have eyes. I know who you are" then he abruptly turned and left. His ambiguous statement sounded like a cautionary remark that left me uneasy and with an uncanny feeling that I was being observed without my knowledge. The ominous warning from Azman resurfaced in my mind. I let the sisters know of my misgivings.

"Do not worry, he sees how kind you are to us. He likes you."

I learned from Faridah that this man, the strangest I had ever come across, was Ayoh-ha, the caretaker of the house. Only later did I find out that he was also a *bomoh*, a Malay-Muslim healer and shaman. To this day, he remains an enigmatic figure for me and I feel uncertain of his identity or his real place in the scheme of things. However, it was from him that I would receive the first inkling of the inner history of the house, and it was he who initiated me into its hidden dimensions.

It had to be a matter of time that a proper introduction to the shaman could happen and it was Faridah who informed me that I was invited to tea with him. Our little conclave would take place a late afternoon in a room used for healing rituals and prayers.

A mist of light welled in through a portal, mirrored by golden hangings and Persian carpets that draped the walls. On the floor, furnished with rattan cane mats throughout, gleamed a round brass tray with two glass teacups and a battered brass teapot. Ayoh-ha sat cross-legged, bolt upright, arms resting lightly on his lap, wrapped in the folds of a white silk sarong. He wore a Javanese batik shirt with a prodigious abstract pattern that, for a second, took the shape of dozens of eyes staring at me at once. I waited for him to choose a cup. He drew it slowly to his fat lips, that looked even bigger through the foot of the glass, took a sip and placed the cup back exactly where it was. The most intriguing man I had ever met sat now opposite me and I had no idea what to say. Words were not out of our mouths, but there was a conversation to follow in his motions, carried with extreme parsimony and decorum, as if every little thing he did was a subtle message I was supposed to read. My camera was close at hand, but I waited patiently until he nodded his consent for me to take his portrait.

To illustrate the endeavours of his line of work, Faridah came to translate from Malay a brief story about one of those people who requested his services.

Salibah was a woman from Gua village whose husband had not been home for several days. She had no doubts that he had sneaked out on her to be with his young minor wife. She wanted him back. Ayoh-ha cast a spell using some of the husband's personal belongings soaked in water and jasmine rice. The shaman predicted he would be back home after three days. It was agreed that three carpets would be given as payment for the services.

Three days later Salibah's husband returned home. This fact was confirmed by the neighbours, who happened to know the shaman. However, whether out of negligence or deception, Salibah failed to keep her end of the bargain. A few days later, she was riding on her motorbike in the border town of Betong when her mind went blank and ploughed into a parked car. She broke both of her legs. She could not find a reasonable explanation for the cause of the accident. The street was ample and there was no traffic. The car was right there in front of her, yet she hadn't seen it. Ayoh-ha took a sip of tea and concluded, "That is the price to pay if you lie to a *bomoh*."

* * *

One day, Irfan, Fatimah's youngest son, fell ill with fever and joint pain, suggesting seasonal flu. I did not worry unduly as after a week the boy was getting better. However, one morning, I found him lying on a mat, wrapped in several layers of quilts, soaked in sweat from a high fever. His mother sat beside him, gently dabbing his brow with a wet cloth. His condition had worsened with nausea, vomiting and backache, symptoms that could relate to any number of tropical diseases with serious consequences. Not wanting to sound alarmist, I offered a few words of encouragement, but with the conviction that without proper medical care, the boy would probably get worse.

My fears turned into reality when Fatimah became so worried that she sent for her husband. However, as this was the week he spent with his first wife, he declined to come. His disregard for his own son seemed cold and uncaring, but I said nothing. Neither Fatimah nor Faridah suggested taking the boy to the hospital. Knowing they had little money and that the cost of treatment would be an issue, I was tempted to offer help, but unsure of how this might be received by Fatimah's husband, I chose to wait and see. At a loss as to what else to do, Fatimah asked Ayoh-ha to use his healing powers on her son.

Ayoh-ha sat behind Irfan and began whispering a sort of chant, his fingers turning over the beads of a rosary while swaying slightly from side to side. We all waited in silent expectation. As dusk fell, darkness began to flow in from outside and by the time

Ayoh-ha had finished, shadows encompassed the hall. Irfan was seated, with Fatimah and Faridah on either side clasping his hands to hold him upright. His eyelids were drooping and his head sagged. Ayoh-ha placed his right hand wrapped with prayer beads on the boy's back, closed his eyes and began chanting incantations in Malay. The *bomoh* paused at times to blow a long, powerful breath onto his neck. The session lasted about 20 minutes and, at its end, Irfan burst into a wail of pain and tears that shattered the serenity in the house. It almost broke my heart.

Fatimah enfolded her son in her arms before he collapsed on the floor. Seeming calmer, he was made to lie down on the mat, cuddled lovingly by his mother. Everyone presumed that the healing spells had been successful and that the boy was through the worst. Ayoh-ha lit a cigarette and leaning his elbow on his leg, stared at Irfan, smoking with a contented smile. Faridah, cloaking herself in a yellow veil, fetched a glass of water over which she whispered words for a few minutes, before handing it to Irfan to drink. When I left the house, the boy was quietly asleep.

That week, Irfan seemed to get better. His fever nearly gone, he was in the mood to play with his brothers, until one afternoon I found Fatimah deeply distressed. To my dismay, her son's condition had deteriorated rapidly and, this time, he could no longer eat. Beside him, darker than the enveloping shadows, was the prostrate figure of an old woman swathed in a black niqab, holding his hand tenderly. It was his anxious grandmother who had rushed from Yala. Greeting her with a smile that tried to convey reassurance, she looked up at me. I could hardly see her eyes, buried in a face furrowed by a life of toil. I sat alongside her grandson and carefully laid my palm on his forehead. His fever was blazing, his eyes glazed. That morning, Irfan started to groan, twitching and outreaching his arms as if straining to grab something invisible, labouring in a fit of delirium that occurs before someone slips into a coma. I feared he would not survive another night without medical care. Fatimah was expecting her husband but he hadn't appeared yet. Meanwhile, the sisters' father arrived from Sisakorn. He was a slim and quiet man with a slow and deliberate gait due to his prosthesis, fitted after his leg had been amputated at the knee following a severe viper bite while clearing shrubs on a rubber plantation years ago. He and his wife were separated and did all they could to stay away from each other even under these difficult circumstances.

I could bear it no longer and urged Fatimah to take her son to the hospital right away. She and the other members of her family were reluctant to do this but finally accepted my help. Just then, Fatimah's husband arrived who fortunately also agreed. There were no vehicles available so I phoned a friend who was a volunteer ambulance driver in town to take Irfan to the hospital. We spent that night there. It turned out that he was suffering from dengue fever, which could have been fatal if not treated in time.

Unfortunately, I was due to be back in Bangkok soon for work, and with the boy still hospitalised, I announced my departure to the family.

* * *

"When are you coming back?" the sisters asked. I did not really know. Their eyes and the tone of their question conveyed resignation. This foreigner, who had participated in a short chapter of their lives, would soon leave and become a memory. The day before my departure, Fatimah handed me a letter addressed, "To our dear brother." It was beautifully written in Thai, and they had made a great effort to include some English sentences to express their gratitude, friendship and love. I kept it folded in the pages of my journal.

During my days in Bangkok, when a yearning for the south gnawed at me, I found comfort reading their letter again. My adventures riding through the border provinces, the old-fashioned aura of Narathiwat, the solitude and silence in the House of the Raja and the moments I had spent with the family would then revisit me as dreamlike images. These visions often accompanied me when I walked through the bustling streets, shedding a light on the absurdity of city life that made me feel apart from the hordes on cramped pavements, from the accretion of glass and concrete that obliterated the sky, and from the drivers languishing slowly along overflowing roads.

Nevertheless, the city finally sucked me in. All I could do was garrison myself in my apartment and digest what I had experienced in the south. Most Bangkok residents had never been there, knew nothing about it and did not really want to know. For them, the names Yala, Pattani and Narathiwat are ominous words conjuring up chaos and death. The journey had aroused in me an urge to learn about the region, its past and its people.

I began perusing chronicles, annals and essays to find that this forsaken land had once been the cradle of one of the earliest Southeast Asian civilisations. I spent sleepless nights reading, my imagination disinterring spirit lands, epic warriors and legendary kings and queens until the city outside faded behind a mirage of forgotten worlds that only lifted with the break of dawn. I had never been so captivated by history.

I discovered that the conflict in the south sprung from far earlier than just a decade, when Narathiwat, along with the other southern provinces, comprised the Malay Kingdom of Patani, ruled by puissant Muslim Queens named after the colours of the rainbow, inheritors of a land of magic and gold, coveted in times past by every empire in Asia: the fabled Kingdom of Langkasuka.

THE SPELL OF
LANGKASUKA

~II~

My return to Narathiwat was on a bright afternoon in early April at the peak of the hot season, the sky an unsullied ocean hovering aloft. I headed with joy to the Bang Nara Hotel, checked in to the same river-view room and retrieved my bicycle from storage. It felt like coming home. The only apparent change was the new staff in charge of the hotel, a young married couple from Chumphon who had left their six-year-old daughter in the care of her grandmother. When I asked about the state of affairs in town, the wife replied matter-of-factly, "Nothing, as usual," but after I kept asking why they had left their daughter behind, she shouted as if the answer was all too obvious, "It's dangerous around here!"

On my way upstairs, I found some of the women sitting in a circle on the landing around a huge pile of condom strips. They were cutting them off one by one and putting them into a big bowl. One of them handed me a few as a "welcome gift" and said with a naughty smile, "Would you like to try them? The hospital gives them away for free."

Upstairs, the door to Peter's room was open and I found him stretched out, enjoying a siesta on his bed, lulled by the static from his out-of-tune radio. Later I was dismayed to learn that a motorbike had hit him while crossing the street and that the accident had damaged his hip replacement.

I left my backpack in my room and went out on the balcony to see the river. Above, a sea eagle glided on the breeze of the gulf and across the silky waters of the Bang Nara. I breathed in the azure, the greenery and the small mountain beyond.

Next morning, I skipped breakfast to set out early for Kampung Takok, thrilled at the prospect of seeing the family at the house. The sun was climbing higher and the haze that concealed the lower reaches of the mountain had already evaporated. I made my way at a leisurely pace, cycling through the oldest streets of the town, where low-rise clusters of wooden shophouses stood with folding timber doors, painted sky blue, yellow or lime green. Flocks of swifts swirled over the tiled roofs, screeching as they swooped in and out of the upper floor of *Baan Burong*, a century-old Sino-Portuguese mansion now used as a bird's-nest house[6].

Beyond the esplanade to my left, a silvery thread of the Bang

---

6 Building used for edible-nest swiftlet farming. The birds build nests of their saliva, believed by the Chinese to have both aphrodisiac and medicinal properties. It ranks amongst the world's most expensive animal products.

Nara River shimmered with the morning blaze. Across the street, students in tidy white and navy-blue uniforms swarmed into an elementary school under the watch of armed militiamen garbed in camouflage fatigues. The weather was much hotter than three months earlier. Halfway to the house and past the park, I started to sweat. It was only then that the thought arose that dramatic changes could have taken place while I was absent; that the family might no longer live in the house; or worse, that the building had yielded to the weight of time and finally collapsed.

My ominous thoughts subsided as I reached the small mosque in Kampung Takok. It was somehow reassuring to see the same elders who always whiled away on a bench after prayers watching the passers-by. They greeted me cheerfully, asking me where I had been and what I had been doing while away. One of them drew himself up with a grin, earnestly clasped my hand and, keen to show off his English, went so far as to say, "I love you!" I followed his cue replying, "I love you, too!" Most of the locals knew a few words of English, often picked up from movies and, without knowing their exact meaning, used them eagerly at every opportunity to greet foreigners. Even shouting "Go away!" was regarded as a warm welcome.

The house was indeed still there, slumped between overhanging trees, radiating the same timeless presence. For a moment, while staring at its forlorn figure, I had the impression of being welcomed by the wan voice of an old friend who had been waiting for me after a long separation.

I made my way to the verandah and, to my relief, saw familiar sandals scattered on the floor. One of the double doors was open. Inside, in the shade of the far end of the foyer, the two sisters were having a meal with their children. I stood under the archway, watching them in silence until they became aware of me.

The sisters leapt to their feet, shouting joyfully, "We have missed you!" Irfan, now recovered, ran to embrace me and lovingly gave me the Thai "nose kiss" on my cheek. The rest of the children hugged me warmly. Only Waesuraini, Faridah's daughter, was too shy to approach, now unaccustomed to my presence. Ayoh-ha, the *bomoh*, came later towards noon, clad entirely in white for Friday prayers. We clasped both hands and he smirked at me as if to say, "I knew you would come back."

I found a few changes; the cooking area had been moved out to the foyer because the room that used to hold it was falling apart. Also, one of the rooms adjacent to the central hall had been arranged to accommodate Beraheng, the sisters' father, who had left the solitude of his jungle home in Sisakorn to stay with his daughters and grandchildren for a few weeks. In spite of his bad leg, Beraheng displayed no signs of self-pity but had a dignified composure that suited the lost grandeur of the place. Finding shelter from the heat in a corner, he would settle in silence with his prayer beads and his box of *rokok daun*, the traditional Malay palm-leaf cigarette, and let time pass by, smoking away, one roll after another. Sometimes his gaze would go vacant and stern, as if something was weighing on his mind. He was not talkative and spoke Thai with a heavy accent – he had learned it from his daughters – so our chats were scant and short. Nevertheless, on a couple of occasions he offered me a hint of fellowship, clasping my arm while a wide grin replaced his usual austere look.

Soon, my daily visits, the games with the children, the baths and meals and my wanderings around the building made me feel like I had never left. The children chased me everywhere, euphoric, shouting my name again and again. Little Waesuraini loved to jump on my back and hang from my neck while I ran around playing horse until I became exhausted. Irfan would grab my forearm and demand to be lifted in the air. I would then scoop him up in both arms as if to hurl him out of a window, shouting, "I'll throw you away!" Whenever I did this he laughed gleefully and always asked for more.

Montri and Pantawon, overwhelming me with their teenage curiosity, were convinced I knew the answers to all their questions. They had an aptitude for art and always keenly showed me their drawings and clay models. Montri certainly had an eye for composition so I taught him how to use my camera and a few times even let him carry it around to take photographs by himself.

The century-old vintage safe with a combination lock I had seen the first time I came to the house was still there. Caked with rust, it looked so sturdy and thick that it might as well have weighed a ton, and was probably the only reason why thieves had not bothered to take it away. On its door was a plaque that said, "Manufactured by J. Grove & Son, Birmingham, England". It used to sit in a corner, but according to Faridah, had been moved by Ayoh-ha himself, employing prodigious strength at his command. Now, the safe stood against one of the columns in the central hall like Pandora's box, not to be opened again.

The children clustered around me as I proceeded to inspect the safe. The backside, partially visible, was bent and damaged by corrosion, most likely forced open by a burglar long ago. Pantawong, who had a predisposition for the adventurous, lit up a match and looked closely through the gap. "I see something!"

The gap was very narrow, but wide enough for Waesuraini to put her little hand in. She groped her way inside until we heard her shouting, "I got it!" She pulled out her arm, holding a rectangular object that she placed on the mat. It was a tin cigarette box. On the lid, behind a cloud of rust, was the word "PIRATE" and, just below appeared a warrior wearing a horned moustache, attired in traditional Malay costume with a kris dagger under his sash, one hand on his hip and the other resting on the pommel of a scimitar.

"Ayoh-ha!" claimed Pantawong. The children were in awe.

In my wishful imagination, inside the box there would have been stowed documents waiting to unveil the most recondite memories of the house. But when we opened it all we found was a stack of trade cards of yesteryear illustrated with animals that paraded like humans, walking on two legs: a fox in a top hat carrying a briefcase; a stork with a monocle and smoking a cigar; a camel with a bindle over his shoulder; a frog wearing patent leather shoes, carrying a walking stick and clutching a bankroll in his hands; and a rat dressed like a tramp. The children were delighted at the discovery of this piece of British Malaya memorabilia.

Once, I asked permission from the sisters to take their children along with some of their neighbour friends to the beaches of Ao Manao. We all went on bicycles, swapping silly jokes and puzzling the soldiers posted at the army checkpoint across the river bridge. In the safety of a sheltered cove, I taught them how to swim. Little Waesuraini refused to join in, and sat on the shore pouting. Standing in the shallows, but still beyond their depth, I beckoned them one at a time to overcome their fear and reach me. Thrilled at their feat, they would take refuge for a minute by slinging their arms around my neck to regain their strength before swimming back to the shore.

I spent as much of the day as possible in the house, always leaving with just enough time to reach my hotel before its doors shut. Ayoh-ha came every morning, only to leave at intervals between prayers at the mosque. Faridah told me that he usually left late to return home to his wife who lived nearby. His mother also lived in the neighbourhood. One afternoon, the children took me to meet them.

Ayoh-ha's house was a tiny shack of wood and tin. His 70-year-old wife was handicapped, and spent her days alone, lying down with bleary eyes by the doorway. I saw her full of life only once, when she sat up aiming a slingshot with a determined grimace at an intruding cockerel and scored a direct hit. Whenever I visited her, she received me with a sweet smile but her face always turned grim when asking me about Faridah. During one of my visits, she dragged herself to reach for an old black-and-white photograph of herself. She wanted to show me the beautiful woman she had once been. Putting in a great deal of effort, she made herself up, put on her bonnet and sat up, holding the portrait in her hands and asked me to take a picture, as if the youth in that image could momentarily be reborn in her. I could do no more than sit next to this lonely wife, offering my company and attention for some time, no matter how banal our conversation.

Next door in another shack lived Ayoh-ha's mother. Tiny and thin, I often found her sitting next to her only window, reading the Qur'an with a pointer stick that seemed a prolongation of her woody fingers. Despite being 100 years old, she was healthy and had an incredibly lucid mind. She was born when Narathiwat still bore its old name, Bang Nara, and could not speak Thai. She belonged entirely to the Malay world. As she sat gracefully with an arresting presence at odds with the humbleness of her home, I could see much of her in Ayoh-ha: his features, the ceremony of his gestures and the intriguing self-assurance in his eyes, sombre and gripping at the same time. I perceived in her that same ancient and obscure world of the *bomoh*, so alien to mine. Despite the vast distance between our worlds, my relationship with Ayoh-ha, "your father" as Faridah later called him, would become much closer than I could ever anticipate.

* * *

He was a vital man, with a beefy physique that exuded a thick scent of earth and wood. His character was a strange blend of different personae and demeanours. In one minute, he might be a brute, then a joker, a child, a patriarch, a demon, a mentor, a madman. Ayoh-ha could be any one of the several spirits that protected the Rumoh Rajo, and harness their various powers at his behest to heal, acquiring the might of a tiger, the senses of a serpent, or the strength of an elephant. It was said that he could invoke rain. Although 76, he looked 20 years younger. Perhaps he fooled death with his charms. Always wrapped in a sarong, often with a naked torso, he sat with his thick legs crossed over each other, so overstretched that they looked detached from the rest of his body. Concealed under his sarong, he wore a thin leaf girdle with ancient silver coins and tiny lumps of petrified wood girded around his waist as a shield against evil. Six rings bulged out from his fingers, finely carved in silver and crowned with emerald and ruby stones that possessed hidden properties and the power to summon the other world. But the most intense power emanated from his mouth, from his breath, from his words, able to sway both spirits and mortals. He sat ceremoniously addressing those around him from an invisible pulpit, declaiming stories and myths that enthralled, words oozing from his dark lips that kept listeners spellbound, seeping by osmosis through their skin and deep down into their entrails. Sometimes when I was alone with him, he would draw close to me, his stare cast on some object he rolled in his fingers, muttering cryptic obscenities and commands that always ended with, "I speak the truth, believe me" – words that always left me unsettled.

The mischievous persona in Ayoh-ha could pop up without notice, blurting some obscure word at me and following it up with a penetrating stare. Instead of asking him what that word meant, I would just repeat it, because it seemed that that was what he expected me to do and an explanation would surely follow. Instead, he would reply with the same word, this time placing greater emphasis on it and I echoed him in turn, trying to mouth the right pronunciation. He would utter it again even louder and I would echo him, and before I knew it I had turned into a parrot, caught in an infinite loop of one-word dialogue. The spiral would go on and on with Ayoh-ha's laughter reverberating through the hall, arousing my suspicion that this was but a prank by the unruly child in him to make me speak profanities in Malay. In an instant, though, the serene *bomoh* returned and he would become quiet and serious as if nothing had been said, leaving the actual meaning of the word just one more of his mysteries.

Faridah and Ayoh-ha had a strong bond, the nature of which was hard to understand. It was one that certainly did not exist between him and Fatimah. I only unravelled a bit more of this relationship when I learned that yet another sister, the youngest, was in fact married to Ayoh-ha's eldest son. The couple had been living in the house until two years ago when family dissensions prompted them to move out and live in the border town of Tak Bai. The family ties, as well as Faridah's vulnerability as a Muslim single mother in need of a patron, could have explained the mutual closeness and complicity between her and the *bomoh*. One day, when I irrupted in Farida's room, I found her lying down beside Ayoh-ha with her head on his bare chest, both apparently asleep. Then, as I was going to turn back, she opened her eyes and, at seeing me, quickly straightened herself up. This only reinforced my suspicions that they might be lovers, but I intuited that there was something else, deeply rooted in a past they both secretly shared. Whatever it was, it had joined Faridah to Ayoh-ha, as his protégée, his acolyte in rituals and faithful advocate in the house. The Rumoh Rajo was much more than their home; it was their natural realm, their source of power and their sanctuary and they had become the avatar of the house, its voice and the guardians of its misty past.

I rarely asked questions and preferred to listen to whatever was said about the past, but, as the weeks went by, I felt confident enough to be more inquisitive. Faridah was always very helpful at elucidating in Thai the accounts from Ayoh-ha in Malay, often accompanied with eloquent gesticulations and imbued with fantastical elements entwined with truth. I could never be sure of their veracity. I listened to his descriptions of how the house must have been in its heyday and to his portrait of the Raja who, according to the *bomoh*, had two long black hairs that sprouted up from his throat, a unique trait of those with innate magic powers, which he used to transform his swordstick into a snake. Listening to Ayoh-ha was like leafing through an old book and reading whatever page fell open at random. Over the months, and in a piecemeal fashion, the story of the house emerged. I assembled those many fragments into the following account:

The full name for the building in vernacular Malay was 'Rumoh Rajo Legeh' – The House of the Raja of Legeh. The age of the original construction was uncertain, but could date hundreds of years based on the pillars that bore the front wing. An architect from Terengganu renovated the mansion sometime during the 19th century. It used to have dozens of rooms and was once part of a compound that stretched from the riverbank to where the current clock-tower is located, encompassing other residential buildings for relatives, guests, retinue and commanders, barracks quarters for the *Askar*, the Raja's guard, and in the outer area a plaza, a bullfight arena, elephant stables and sapodilla and pomegranate orchards.

The house had been the residence of the Raja and his family, the well and bath pools in the courtyard used exclusively by them. A total of seven wells scattered across the property supplied with water to other buildings. The compound had its own riverfront market and a jetty with a pavilion at the end, where cargo vessels from Singapore docked to load cattle and coconut, and from where ships sailed upstream all the way to Kelantan.

The Raja of Legeh had a Chinese wife with whom he had no offspring. He raised several children given to him in adoption, his favourite being a Caucasian boy called Jeh Puteh, which in Malay means "white commoner". Three years before Japanese paratroopers descended upon Narathiwat to invade Malaya, the Raja died, leaving the care of his residence to Jeh Puteh. Shortly after the war, the Raja's heirs, whose aristocratic background had exempted them from work, sold their parcels of the land alongside the riverbank to a rich Chinese merchant. Most of the compound's buildings were later torn down to build the coconut warehouse that remains standing behind the house today. Only the Rumoh Rajo survived. During the construction of the warehouse, the workers who tried to demolish the wall that safeguarded the residence died as result of sudden internal haemorrhages.

The young Ayoh-ha paid frequent visits to the house and forged a close friendship with Jeh Puteh, who entrusted his friend with the responsibility to find him an appropiate wife. Ayoh-ha eventually married one of the Raja's adopted granddaughters and lived together in the house until something made him leave Narathiwat hastily.

He would not return for 30 years (he was vague about this gap in his life).

After Jeh Puteh died, the household became a burden to maintain. In time, relatives and servants had all left. Only a midwife from the Raja's original retinue called Moh Nah stayed in a last bid to keep a houseful of memories alive. The old woman lived alone in the palace for years, in the course of which both slowly withered together until, overcome by illness, she had to move out to live with her adopted daughter. But the house was still inhabited. The midwife had been secretly nursing a ghost child and locals who approached the abandoned building to make a surreptitious visit would hear an eerie voice crying out from the shadows, "Mother, where are you? I am hungry..."

The house was left forsaken for many decades and soon gained a reputation as being cursed. People attested to seeing a giant snake that glided out of the building. Yet, another even more fearful creature dominating the foyer to ward off unwanted visitors was the 'Raja Burong', a giant carved bird's head with a tusked beak made of wood, gold and ivory, adorned with jewelled plumes, velvet and silk feathers. A symbol of the ruler's power and dynastic prestige, this head formed part of a lofty winged chariot on which the Raja would sit under a double-tiered wood canopy on important ceremonial occasions. It was also upon this token that in the old days propitiatory Malay rituals and trials by ordeal were staged in the palace. A defendant would be instructed to extract an egg previously inserted in the bird's beak. If he were unable to remove it he would be declared guilty of his alleged crime and, in severe cases, sentenced to death with the Raja's kris (a prized Malay dagger). Thereupon, he was ordered to kneel down and a cotton wool would be placed on his shoulder. The executioner would stand behind him, holding the royal kris perfectly vertical, the point of its blade resting next to the neck of the condemned, just behind the collar bone. Then, upon the signal from the Raja, the blade was driven downward with a quick thrust deep into the heart. This technique allowed for a less sanguinary execution compared to that of decapitation.

Fearing ill consequences if the totem was snatched from the Rumoh Rajo, the Raja's heirs had not dared to remove the 'Raja Burong', but, apprehensive that it might fall into the wrong hands, they decided to take it away only after performing a complicated precautionary ritual. The 'Raja Burong' was never to be seen again (latest rumours place it lodged in a museum in Kuala Lumpur).

Although divested of its protective talisman, the house still hosted invisible, yet powerful forces. Nightmares or unnatural maladies would torment those outsiders reckless enough to overnight in the building. Only those wicked enough to act under the safeguard of black magic managed to loot it.

After decades of absence, Ayoh-ha returned to Kampung Takok to find to his dismay that the building was dilapidated, its treasures plundered. Consternated by the state of neglect, he resolved to repair it as much as he could and make it habitable once more. He cleaned up the debris accumulated underneath and around the building, replaced broken boards, wall panels and stair planks on lower and upper floors, although without the means to restore its original cengal or meranti wood. He also climbed down the courtyard well to remove the sediments that clouded the water and make it drinkable again.

All that remained from the time of the Raja were his clothes and his notable *destar*[7], which no one had the nerve to touch after two male relatives of the Raja who tried wearing them died in mysterious circumstances. Only Ayoh-ha proved able to put them on without being harmed. One day, while he was trying to rekindle remembrances by parading around in the Raja's clothes, Jeh Puteh's widow coincidentally visited. She took Ayoh-ha for the Raja returned from the dead and swooned at his sight, dying a few days later.

Ayoh-ha overnighted in the house under feeble candlelight,

---

7 According to Malay legend, Sultan Muzaffar, the son of the last ruler of Malacca who fled the Portuguese, was sailing to Perak to form his new sultanate, when his ship, overloaded with many of the royal regalia of the Malacca Sultanate, ran aground in shallow waters. Only after offering the Royal Crown of Malacca to the sea would the ship budge. The Sultan, seeing the miracle as a sign, swore that he and his descendants would never wear a crown as sultans. Since then, *destar* would be the royal head-dress worn by Malay Rulers, made of embroidered silk folded in different styles.

penumbras his only companions. During a full moon, he slept in the attic. His grandfather, a pawang[8] whose long lineage extended far into the rainforests of Java, visited him in dreams as real as experiences in the flesh. In one of them, he sat in a cave in Bukit Tanjong with an old hermit famed for his ability to manipulate fire. As Ayoh-ha's grandfather drew a palm cigarette, the hermit offered him light taking a flame from the bonfire with his hand. "How come you can do that?" the shaman asked. Then his grandfather untied his turban and wound it around the flame, without the slightest singe. To this, the hermit responded "You are more powerful than I am." That very night Ayoh-ha was endowed with the ability to invoke the supernatural. Embedded in the Rumoh Rajo, his skills developed as occasional dreams revealed further knowledge to him and he began to receive those fated to meet the newcomer *bomoh*.

As I listened to him, trying to picture the young Ayoh-ha in my mind, it was apparent that not only was he withholding much about the house, but also about his past. Most of the story seemed to be more a product of his imagination than an actual account. That the house had been the palace of a late Raja could be also a fantasy, but I found myself without resources at my disposal to refute it. There was little else I could do aside from listening to him like a child and let his words flow without judging them. I began to wish someone could help me separate myth from facts, someone with whom I could share my fascination with the house.

---

8 A medicine man said able to control the elements and wild animals by having spirit servants to do his bidding.

* * *

Nightly entertainment choices in town were scarce. Somewhat removed from the centre and near the provincial hospital were the gaudy karaoke bars, festooned with strings of fairy lights that seemed to announce a premature Christmas. Curiosity drew me there once, but after boring exchanges with a few girls and being harassed by a drunken soldier who took a fancy to my cheap watch, I vowed not to return. Then there was Tango, a tacky nightclub in a mid-range hotel frequented by prostitutes. The girls swayed on the dance floor in a desultory fashion to ear-piercing Thai pop music while drunken men tottered and staggered around trying to woo them. I had fun watching the show once, but could not bear it twice.

My favourite hangouts were where most locals spent the leisurely hours between last prayers and sleep, the *kedai kopi* or tea shops. After the mosques, the *kedai kopi* were the pillars of social life in town, where people came to chat, gossip, plot and argue and were the best places not only to make new contacts but also to build close friendships, all furnished with endless rounds of luscious egg and curry roti and tea.

My habitual tea shop was close to an old mosque across from the clock-tower and next to a roti stall owned by a good Malay friend of mine. Stocky and frank-speaking, Ju hawked what he proudly claimed to be the only coconut-stuffed roti in town. He was the ambulance driver who had brought Irfan to the hospital a few months earlier. Besides volunteering for a rescue group, he occasionally worked as a wedding photographer. We met at the photo shop where I used to print my pictures and often asked me for advice on how to improve his camera skills. Always eager to introduce me to others in his circle, one day he insisted I should meet another amateur photographer friend of his.

Abdul Hannan, a 32-year-old Malay born in Yakang, a village on the outskirts, taught history at a government high school in town. I liked him at once. Whenever something sparked his interest, his amber eyes lit up and smiled with the naivety of a child showing his teeth above an unobtrusive goatee. Besides Malay and Thai, he knew Arabic and could speak out-of-practice English. We talked mostly in Thai but he was always keen to use his vocabulary to translate whatever word I did not understand from Thai to English and vice versa. Though I kept forgetting those words again and again, he never failed to repeat his explanations, and it is to him that I owe a lot of the improvement in my language skills.

The eldest son of a respected Imam at Darulkhoar mosque in Yakang village, Hannan was expected to fulfil his father's wish for him to be a teacher and although he had been teaching for nearly five years, he still cherished his own dreams. Hannan valued his work as an educator, aware of the impact he could make on the future of his students, but he felt often frustrated with the curriculum and methods imposed from the capital, which he found obsolete or illogical. Among those rules was the task of teachers to overnight in the school as a watchman twice every month, a job without remuneration considered by the board of directors not so much as a duty, but as an honour and a voluntary act of love for the institution. His efforts to introduce improvements in the school always confronted the wariness of the principal who regarded the capability in this young subordinate as a threat to his authority and position.

Hannan endured his occupation with forbearance, dreaming of devoting himself to something that allowed putting into practice his ideas. Meanwhile, part-time graphic design assignments and photography kept his creative aspirations alive. With time, I developed a great affinity for this young man who, like me, also loved the arts. Despite his family duties, I felt that Hannan was a free spirit with the soul of an artist. Non-conformist and intelligent, he was the only person I found in town with whom I could have a heart-to-heart chat about the subtle aspects of life and human nature. For his part, Hannan was intrigued to see how a Westerner looked at the world and particularly the land where he was born. Many of our conversations revolved around how photography was about seeing, rather than taking, the enriching experience of travelling, the cultural differences between the West and the East and just about everything else except religion, unless I was the one who brought it up. However, this was not from a real reluctance on his part. A passionate believer of Islam as a concept that should not necessarily impugn vernacular culture, he was happy to share his knowledge of Islamic teachings, and he did this without any proselytising. Rather, he carried his religion in his heart and placed friendship above all else. I felt at home with him.

When I met Hannan again at Ju's roti stall, I began to tell him about the house, the family and Ayoh-ha. The history teacher was amazed to hear from a foreigner something about his hometown of which he was unaware. Intrigued by my descriptions, he asked to meet me again and see the photographs I had taken.

Hannan lived in a nearby shophouse across from an old Muslim cemetery and west of the clock-tower. His wife, Pu, from Chiang Mai, had met him while studying history at the Pattani Campus of Prince of Songkhla University and had converted from Buddhism to Islam before they married. They had lived in Bangkok, where there were better job opportunities, until she got pregnant and then moved to raise their children in the more placid Narathiwat. The couple had a girl and a boy, who unfortunately had a congenital disability that made it difficult for him to walk, although he seemed to be improving slowly after undergoing surgery several times.

That evening, as we went through the photographs, his eyes glistened. "I was there once, many years ago!" Hannan exclaimed, astonished. Ten years earlier, his former high school art teacher, an artist called Zakariya, who was researching Malay architecture, had requested his assistance in photographing an old building that had some interesting features.

They found the building closed up and uninhabited, overrun by trees and shrubs, rubble piled underneath over years of abandonment. A dusky old woman in a frayed sarong gave them a jolt when she emerged from a hut adjacent to the mansion, "Why you come here?" she hollered, looking hard at them. The teacher managed to appease her, explaining that this was an educational outing for his student and that they would leave soon. When they were out of her sight, Hannan and Zakariya clambered among the many pilars under the structure, crawling over a heap of timber and planks to emerge through the central part of the collapsed floor. Inside, they found themselves in a bare hall where two crossed spears hung on a wall. Leaning against a corner, misted by the light falling from a window, sat a tall, old-fashioned safe eaten by rust. He wondered what was inside. Treading carefully on parts of the flooring, they reached several doors that gave onto empty rooms, except one that was tightly bolted. They ventured further into the back hall where two stairways led to the attic. Hannan suggested going up, but Zakariya refused without explanation and asked him to take photos of some architectural details. Perhaps his teacher had been up there before, he thought.

Perched on a wall was a circular frame carved in wood. It was hollow, a mirror missing. Hannan could not resist taking it down to look at the floral motifs that graced the contour. Leaves curled and stalks interlaced, beckoning him in a soothing manner. He was about to put the object in his bag when Zakariya told him with a sour look to put it back up.

After half an hour, the teacher was becoming anxious to leave. Neighbours had told him of a giant serpent, most likely a python that, in the past, had been fed by the Raja and which was said to dwell in one of the wells. Now, the locals believed it was a guardian spirit that shielded the house from intruders. The two made for the exit and agreed on meeting again to get prints of the photos.

Back at his home, Hannan examined the mirror frame. While his teacher had been engrossed in his notes, he had had the gall to take it down again on the quiet. It looked even more beautiful now, with him thinking it would make a nice gift to his wife. He wrapped it in cloth and put it away in his drawer. That night, a growing anguish kept him awake. It was not just regret for having stolen from that house, but remorse amplified to excruciating levels. His wife was in a deep sleep, oblivious to his torture.

He got up and went to the living room to take a look at the frame. It was inconceivable that this would alleviate his pain, but he did not know what else to do. He turned on the lights and unwrapped the frame, only to find that now its mirror was back in place. This was impossible. He stood dumbfounded with drowsy eyes staring himself in the mirror. Wait a minute, he thought. Shouldn't those letters on my shirt appear backward? Was his own mind playing tricks on him? Then it hit him that this was not himself looking at his reflection. This was, actually, the other way around. He was the reflection itself, looking at his own person, not from behind or in front of the mirror, but from *within* the molecular interstice in the glass. His other self did not seem to notice the bizarre phenomenon at all. His face did not show the slightest sign of emotion, like that of a mannequin. But the more he looked to this hollow version of himself, the more it seemed to infuse vitality in him, as if the selfhood embed in the mirror, the one with consciousness, was being transferred to his alter ego outside. Then, he saw that the other self opened his mouth and eyes wide open, as if he had gained awareness, and as he did, the sound of cracking glass burst deep into his ears, through his eyes, to the core. He smashed to smithereens. Ceased to exist. Erased.

When he woke to the nightmare, he was panting, his heart racing and wet to the crotch, convinced to have faced death itself.

As dawn broke, he rushed back to the house to put the object of his torment at rest. Alone and without the warming of sunrays, the place felt wintry and stark. The quickest thing would be to slide the frame through the floor crack, but he mustered enough courage to go inside. He slunk across the hall, hung the frame back in its original place and made a bolt for the exit. Just then, he remembered the locked door. Dying of curiosity to see what was on the other side, he climbed to an upper wall to peep through a wooden grille into the room.

A four-poster teak bed draped in golden silk hangings stood awash in shadows. If it were not for the carpet of dust covering the embroidered sheets stretched smoothly over its mattress, one might think somebody had made it up that very morning. But it was evident that no one had lain on that bed for many years. At its foot sat a Victorian steamer trunk and against the opposite wall was a Peranakan dresser and a glass cabinet with Chinese porcelain inside. Hannan had to crane his neck to view a lacquer wardrobe nestled in the right corner. Its doors were ajar, giving a glimpse of clothes neatly folded inside that to all appearances were awaiting their owner's return. Hannan felt shivers run down his spine. He climbed down. Having seen enough and not wanting to push his luck, he slipped through the crack on the floor and swiftly left the place. Over time, Hannan had forgotten about the enigmatic building – until now. During the intervening years, he was unaware of the imprint the house had left on him, as if a kernel of memory had been sown in his mind and lain dormant, waiting for a propitious moment to emerge. Everything I felt about the Rumoh Rajo, its mystery and melancholy, was kindled now in Hannan through the images.

"I have something to show you," he said, jumping up to rummage in a corner through dusty piles of papers and notebooks stored in cardboard boxes.

"Here they are!" he said triumphantly, before returning with a few colour prints.

"These are some of the pictures I took that day," he said, handing them to me. I examined the images carefully. They were close-ups of wood panels, carved in the shape of foliate and floral motifs entwined with curling stems, intricate geometric patterns and delicate Islamic calligraphy, none of them familiar to me. They originally graced ventilation panels on walls, doors and window fanlights, surely one of the most beautiful features of the building. I had noticed that the void left by the panels' removal had been plugged using white plasterboard, corrugated iron sheets and planks that thwarted the path of sunlight. It was obvious that the artwork had been taken away, probably stolen. If only I had arrived earlier, I thought with frustration, as sunlight filtered through those carvings must have woven beautiful shades across the interior. I felt both devastated and angry that the thieves had not only stolen some of the wealth of the palace, but had also denuded part of its soul, the light and shadows that infused life into the building.

"Sorry, but I'm afraid the panels are no longer there," I said handing the prints back to him.

Hannan fell silent for a moment while looking at the photos, apparently assailed by the same regret that had seized me. A twinge of guilt tugged at his conscience as he recalled the mirror frame he had tried to take for himself years ago. However, even though the former palace had been despoiled long before I arrived, it nevertheless retained its spirit and the power to provoke deep emotions and a desire to know more. A name came to my mind: Legeh. It was so often mentioned by Ayoh-ha. Like a spell. Hannan had heard of it from his father, and gathered that it was the name of the supposed Raja, but he knew nothing more.

"If you don't know about your own past, how can you know who you are?" I asked him. I instantly regretted my words, even though they were sincerely aimed at infecting him with my passion. But he was far from offended. He lamented that despite being a native and a history teacher, he actually knew little about his town. That a foreigner showed more interest than him in something that was part of his identity discomfited him further.

He told me that local Malay heritage was rarely treated with either interest or respect, because it was not Thai. In consequence, people in the Deep South, especially the younger generation, knew little about their culture and it was even natural to regard themselves as lowly. There was also a deliberate policy by the government to suppress such knowledge. Part of a campaign to discourage local pride was the official exclusion of the Malay language and parts of history from public schools. Martial law and emergency decree had turned the three provinces into a land where generals swaggered among the local population like warlords, believing they could win the hearts and minds of people with paternalism, doses of patriotic pride and massive budgets at their command. In fact, such measures have produced the opposite effect. The Malays in the south lived in limbo, detached from the Malay world yet estranged within the Thai nation. This was particularly true in the countryside, where people tended to retreat into village life.

"Fear has caused us to shut ourselves off in our own world," Hannan lamented.

The rediscovery of the Rumoh Rajo unlocked a forgotten door that opened onto a wistful past, a past that Hannan was convinced could help people confront their future by being aware of their roots and the olden days, when local communities co-existed in a melting pot of cultures that enriched one another. Without knowing it, that evening Hannan was embarking on a years-long quest.

He began by asking his father, who had heard only that a palace of the Raja of Legeh had once been located in Tanjong Mas. He went next to the elders of his village and began to read as much as he could find, searching out local records. In these tasks he was helped eagerly by his wife Pu, whose English skills were useful in searching foreign sources and in translating materials for me. Hannan also enlisted some of his students to interview older members of their families who might know something of interest. He was so inspired that he even suggested to his school director that the project should be adopted as part of the history curriculum. In this he came up against a barrier he had expected. Not only did the director reject the idea, but Hannan was also warned by his colleagues of the risk of doing fieldwork to look into local history because it could attract the attention of the military, which might see it as part of the separatist movement.

Despite all this, Hannan's passion was stronger than any fears he might have and he refused to give up. Resolved to find out what he could regardless of the consequences, he set about visiting the homes of those who kept artefacts from the old days, or anything else that could shed light on the past. Initially, he met with a general reluctance to rake over the region's turbulent history and a wariness of showing family possessions to strangers, even if they were local Malay-Muslim researchers. Some people still remembered incidents in the past, when villagers had their relics confiscated by soldiers. Surprisingly, Hannan was deemed trustworthy and doors began opening to him even when I joined some of these informal field trips. Ironically my foreign presence did nothing but encourage people to speak out.

Nevertheless, weeks of earnest work uncovered nothing noteworthy on the house apart from the possibility of it having been used as a customs outpost. The rest of his notes were a farrago of irrelevant anecdotes. It was disappointing to think that the house might just have been the summer residence of a merchant or a wealthy family fallen on hard times that had simply passed into local folklore by hearsay, stories in which Ayoh-ha would have been inspired to fabricate his own. I did not believe this hypothesis, however, and convinced as I was of the building's significance, I exhorted Hannan to carry on with his research. I think he was puzzled at my fixation on a rundown mansion that no one else seemed to care about. As silly as it may sound, this puzzled me too. History had never fascinated me to this extent, and, although I had a passion for art and culture, I knew that my obsession had nothing to do with any of those things. It revolved around one thing: the House of the Raja. I was craving to know what had happened to the house and, above all, what had happened to its former owner.

* * *

The next morning, I found Faridah sitting by the entrance as usual, but without the smile she always welcomed me with.

"The soldiers have just been here," she muttered.

Earlier, the family had been resting in their bedrooms when a racket from below startled them. "Come out, come out!" someone shouted, banging hastily on the underside of the floor with a rifle butt. Telling her sister to stay with the children – Ayoha-ha was absent – Faridah put on her veil and hastened out of the room. Outside, a contingent of about 40 soldiers had surrounded the building, their guns at the ready. At their feet were three young men, face-down on the grass, handcuffed behind their back.

She soon realised they were the boys staying in the right wing. Faridah stood in front of the entrance with her arms raised, trying to persuade the soldiers to lower their weapons. A young officer came forward and ordered a squad to search the whole building, while Fatimah, her father and the children were asked to come out of their rooms. The family huddled in a corner of the foyer and remained quiet and watchful, expecting the worst because they knew that under martial law[9], arrests could take place without any need for a court warrant. The officer questioned Faridah about the family's relationship with the boys, demanding to know who the owner of the house was and what the family was doing there. During the search, and adding to the tension, some rotten planks gave way under one of the soldiers, who fell through the floor up to his waist. After the search was over, the soldiers shoved the boys in pick-up trucks and left. Faridah told me the officer had claimed they were involved in illegal drugs.

It was unclear whether the young men who had been living there with Ayoh-ha's permission were narcotic dealers, but whatever the allegations against them, the family was lucky to avoid trouble for harbouring them.

---

9 Prime Minister Thaksin Shinawatra's government imposed three special security laws in the three southern border provinces of Thailand to control the insurgency, namely Martial Law, Emergency Decree and Internal Security Act and the deployment of 150,000 security forces. Martial law, first imposed in 2004, allows soldiers to detain a suspect in any detention place without a court warrant for up to seven days. The Emergency Decree allows up to 30 days of detention without charge in places other than prison. Security forces have used these laws in tandem to hold suspects for 37 days without charge and without presenting a detained person before the court.

Several days after the incident, Faridah's son Pantawong asked me to follow him to look at something. A few weeks earlier, unable to contain his curiosity about the erratic behaviour of the young men, he had plucked up the courage to sneak into their room while they were away. Flashlight in hand, he scouted the place at random, imagining he was a detective probing a crime, until something glinted from beneath a mattress. When he lifted it, a pang of fear twisted his stomach at the discovery of guns and ammunition. It was from this stash, before rushing out of the room, that he took an M-16 round, a memento he had secreted away. I was the only one he had told because he knew I wouldn't get him into trouble.

The disturbing event was soon forgotten, and the room cleared by the army remained vacant. One day I decided to have a look inside with the children. A cow's skull hung on a wall, together with a collection of European football club banners, posters of Thai folk bands and of John Lennon, as well as a peaked cap, a mirror and other paraphernalia scattered on the floor. I was about to leave when Pantawong brought me a notebook he had found tossed in a corner. When I opened it and flicked through pages of what seemed like student profiles, something dropped on the floor – a faded colour photograph of a woman and her son, their faces washed out. On the back was handwritten "1973". Putting the picture back in the notebook, I asked Pantawong to leave it where he had found it. I never went in that room again.

* * *

The curfew at the Bang Nara, once a minor annoyance, was now feeling oppressive. It restricted my time at the house in the evenings and prohibited any prospect of a late-night social life. I had to keep glancing down at my watch, often only to jump up and race back to the hotel if I didn't want to find it shut. Out of exasperation, I started offering small bribes to buy time from the unfriendly housekeeper, the later the hour, the higher the price. She gave me her phone number so that I could ring her to open the gate, but sometimes wouldn't answer my calls and, finding myself stranded in the deserted street, I would resort to banging on the sliding door. Only after I added yelling, would I hear her grumble, before her brisk footsteps approached.

Tired of my troublesome business with the bawd and of always keeping an eye on the time, it had crossed my mind to move into the Rumoh Rajo. It was not my decision to make, but I guess that those things we wish from the heart will sooner or later come to us, often without much exertion on our part.

One evening I was leaving the house reluctantly when Ayoh-ha said out of the blue, "You don't have to come and go. You can come here to stay." My heart leapt with joy at his invitation, but I still had doubts. Once the neighbours became aware that I was staying with the family, word would spread quickly, giving rise to all sorts of speculation. Remembering what had happened months earlier when I contemplated staying overnight, I shared my misgivings with Ayoh-ha. He shrugged them off and said,

"Don't mind what people say, to judge you they have no right."

Both Faridah and Fatimah agreed and encouraged me to accept the invitation, saying that since their father was staying as well, they did not think there was an issue. The decision was made and the next day, I packed and checked out of the hotel, leaving the relative comfort and theatrical mood of the Bang Nara for the alluring, yet obscure, atmosphere of a place whose call I could no longer resist.

My relocation was by no means a matter of simply transferring myself from one building to another. In fact, it felt more like running aground and being shipwrecked.

Faridah showed me to a small, sparse room at the back facing the courtyard. This was not part of the building's original plan but a space that had been screened off as a prayer room cobbled together using recycled parts. The room had a ceiling-high double door that opened onto the courtyard and a window shut with iron sheeting. Just outside was a tiny cement closet with a squat toilet used by the entire house. A wooden rod with wire hangers was the only furniture. My bed was a quilt folded to serve as a mattress, a few mouldy cushions and a moth-eaten coverlet. The only luxury available was a mosquito net I bought at the market to avoid waking up bitten all over. Plastered on each wall, welcomed me in a gibberish of yellowed newspaper scraps in Chinese, Thai, Malay and Hindi, reporting news back from the 70s.

* * *

I always woke in darkness with the first *azan*[10] wafting down from nearby mosques into the house. It helped me to understand how significant the daily cycle of prayers marking the tempo of life was to a Muslim. The calls, heralding the ritual of bathing each time, not only gave a pattern to my days, but also imbued in me a deeper awareness. After dressing, I would get on my bicycle and head to the park in town to exercise. The park, encircled by old banyan trees, was small but well laid out, with lawns, a plaza, vintage wooden benches and two gazebos. Despite still being dark, it was always crowded in the early mornings, with groups of people playing football, jogging round the park, doing aerobics, tai chi or working out along the fitness trail. Muslim women wore their headscarves while exercising and some even wore niqabs. Later, these groups would evaporate as the morning haze gave way to the forenoon heat and then, after an interlude, the very same plaza became a military training ground. Bubbly women in colourful leotards thumping to Thai pop were relieved by fresh militia recruits in camouflage doing their drills under the supervision of stern military instructors.

I would usually return from the park before eight, when the sun's rays began to burn. I undressed, put on my sarong, and headed to the well in the courtyard where, in days gone by, according to Ayoh-ha, only the Raja and his family had had the privilege to

---

10 The Muslim call to ritual prayer typically made by a muezzin from the minaret of a mosque.

bathe. I imagined him sitting wrapped in a silk sarong, while a servant carefully poured a preparation of bathwater infused with fragrant flowers over him. The square brick pool where these rituals presumably took place, stands today crumbling away in a gloomy corner, covered with weeds and occupied by three or four river turtles.

I relished the physical undertaking of bathing: throwing the bucket attached to a cord into the well and hearing the sound of it splashing down in the depths, then hauling it up full of fresh water which I poured slowly over my head, feeling the coolness spreading over my body. During the process, my gaze would wander up to the eaves from which withered vines crept down over the courtyard, to the beams burdened with rot, the spear-like crests struggling to stay upright, and the worn tiles that covered the roof like the petrified skin of an ancient reptile. Bathing amid such decay, the inevitability of decline and death washed over me and I could not help feeling that by being there, I, too, was part of a bygone age. I rejoice in my own mortality. If there is nothing worse than decay and death, how is it then possible that I can find bliss in this edifice of loss?

"When you are part of the routine you are not aware of the change. It doesn't matter where life leads you as soon as you are aware of your impending doom." This was said to me once by Thomas, an old American traveller I had met in the Bang Nara Hotel. He had been a global nomad for years, accompanied by Emma, a Spanish woman who joined him to walk their way through life without aim until the last step. They were convinced that the pursuit of something is burdensome to the mind, that striving to attain things ultimately fails and that the stability of what is considered as a normal life doesn't let our mind settle down by itself, bringing distress, rather than peace. For most of us certainty ought to bring happiness. We want to be certain about everything that happens to us and around us, leaving nothing to the caprices of providence. Certainty seems so ingrained in daily life as to exclude the most uncertain yet inescapable, self-evident truth of our existence, its ending. Of course, we all know that one day we will die. But the moment of our demise from this world appears too far in the future for us to waste time agonising over it or else it weighs too heavily on our minds. We turn away from death. It becomes something unspeakable, frightening, almost unthinkable. Perhaps it is not our fault. Disguised as well-being are the unyielding workings of "modern society", tricking us into forgetting that we originated from the ever-changing natural world, to the point that our sense of belonging falls into the vacuum of our own creation, a world where it is satisfactory to trade freedom for assurance. If certainty doesn't liberate us, then what can make us alive, what can keep our hearts at peace, if not our sensible response to the fact that everything becomes lost to the past?

* * *

My first meal was usually milk coffee, fruit and *nasi kabu*[11], a traditional Malay morning dish consisting of a mixture of bluish

---

11 Called *nasi kerabu* in standard Malay.

rice, raw lemongrass and other herbs, chili and *budu,* a foul-smelling, fermented fish sauce that found its way into most dishes. I became used to its briny taste, but never to its stench. Later in the day, I would have two more baths, the second coinciding with noon prayers before lunch, and the last to mark the formality of going to bed.

Baths and meals; these were the only tokens of earthly life in the house. The intervals of time between – if time can be said to exist in those gaps of suspended nothingness – were filled with contemplative drifts. There was absolutely nothing to do. Nothing was demanded of me, a city-dwelling European, whose social conditioning had forbidden the luxury of just watching life pass by. The house was suspended in its own temporality, a fairyland largely separated from the outside world where mortals continued to wreak havoc and perpetrate their madness and useless killings. Submerged in the profound calm of the space, I was freed from the burden of time or having to make sense of anything and stripped naked of the worry and trivia that used to squash me. I looked at things with different eyes and under this revealing gaze even the dullest corner, the smallest detail, became a fascinating microcosm.

Light and its absence acquired a new dimension, yielding unfathomable qualities and significance as both wafted through the house shifting in shape and intensity, evolving constantly from dawn to dusk, transforming the interior. In the early hours, the first hint of dawn suffused the darkness of my room with a soft, long whisper of velvet blue. As the sun ascended, rays slipped through fissures in the walls, casting thin shafts in which hovering specks of dust glinted as if relaying hidden messages from another world. Outside my room, amber light dappled over the stairways, the flooring and onto the walls; shiny ovals with sharp contours, so bright that they seemed about to ignite the wood on which they alighted, alternating with hazier patches in a gauzy caress.

Tremulous light and shade crept across the halls, cast through carvings and leaves from surrounding trees; luminescent pools gradually paled or even vanished if the sky clouded over, only to reappear the next moment under short spells of sun. In the afternoon, beams reached the hallway, surrendering the rest of the house to the shadows, and then glowing ovals emerged on the floor, ghostly footprints paddling slowly towards the door.

I understood that all those manifestations of light were a flotsam of ancestral recollections resurfacing from the seabed of memory and borne by the tide of time into the present with the passage of the earth around the sun. Adrift in this cyclic wave of memories, I am not able to separate time. For no sooner does future turn to present than present turns to past at once. In the House of the Raja past predates past, over and over again.

Mesmerised by the aging structure, I absorbed myself with the seriousness of a scientist retrieving forensic evidence from the tissue of the wood. My eyes wandered over details as if they were an unmapped treasure, while my fingers stroked textures; the roughness of massive rafters that descended from the ceiling, the powdery touch of crumbling clay tiles, the time-polished surface of ironwood pillars, the round bevel of a lintel above a doorway, or the meanders in the few decorative fretworks that remained. The archaic wood, once the soul of mighty trees in primeval rainforests, perhaps retained its life force and even secrets of its own from ages past that now enchanted me.

Only occasionally did the spell break. At such times, as if awakening from a trance, I would find I had strayed into doubt and confusion, caught in the ebb and flow between opposites – the force that beseeched me to stay in the house and the urge to escape from my isolation. It occurred to me that the peace I had been experiencing was not natural, but rather induced by something beyond my reach that dwelled within the building. I was in a maze in which the longer I stayed, the more oblivious I was to the outside world. Although sometimes I could spur myself to find a way out, it became more and more difficult. I feared that someday I might be unable to find the exit or even grow loath to ever leave. Distressed by this last thought, desperate to escape the suffocating feeling of being marooned, I would rush downstairs, grab my bicycle and peddle off without a word to anyone to seek relief on the quiet beaches of Ao Manao.

* * *

Time itself had thickened, hours drizzling within the walls of the House of the Raja. Somehow, the house had taken a lethargic grip on its inhabitants, holding them in its sway. The family had slipped into inertia and, during my wanderings, I would find them lying here and there, nestled in a shady corner like discarded toys.

One night I suddenly awoke without any apparent reason. Immobile in my bed I could hear a subdued burble that seemed to flow from all corners at once. At first, I mistook it for an illusion of my drowsy mind, but after listening carefully, I discerned a muffled voice that could only be coming from Faridah's room, its timbre familiar.

It was Ayoh-ha.

Strangely, however hard I strained my ears I could not perceive other voices in conversation. Rather, the *bomoh*'s voice flowed in an endless monologue with changing tones, meandering through the mansion, sweeping in and out of rooms and halls, seeking… me? The instant this thought struck me, I plunged back into sleep.

Ayoh-ha had told me that he never went upstairs, so the next morning, when I saw him climbing the stairs with determination, I suspected the unusual. The children also tuned in to this and followed him as I trailed behind. Ayoh-ha trod the attic boards watchfully as if ready for an ambush. He moved erratically while tracing a trail with his index finger, stopping at times here and there as if he were tracking an entity that none of us could hear or see. At one point, he made for the corner, stopped, and then knelt down at a spot where the gable joined the wall. The children and I kept our distance, watching him expectantly without a clue as to the reason for his pursuit. Stretching out his arm he felt along a beam for an invisible object. Suddenly, he left the corner, his hand clenched. Moving into a ray of light slanting through the ceiling he opened his hand.

"I had a dream that told me to come up here and find this," he said. In his palm glittered a tiny round cerulean stone. Although I had no idea of its value, I could see it was beautiful. Saying nothing else, Ayoh-ha pointed to one of the overhead beams. A silky white strip hung down, swaying in the breeze that heaved through the gables. It was a snakeskin.

"A snake lives here," Ayoh-ha proclaimed.

"Is it dangerous?" I asked.

"No. It is a protective being. It had a human shape but now it has become a snake."

"You mean it was a human being before?"

"No. It is a spirit."

To find any relation between the discovery of the stone and the snake seemed an impossible task, but he elaborated further. The snake was a jinn, or what the Muslims call a shape-shifting spirit that inhabits an unseen world of darkness. It is said that every jinn has its human counterpart, so that for every newborn person a jinn is simultaneously begotten. Each one in their world, jinn and humans lead their lives connected by an invisible double-side mirror. The fringes of both worlds only jinn have the faculty to trespass, appearing visible to humans upon their will. Able to incarnate at times in human guise, the jinn in that building demanded respect from visitors and had the power to expel or even inflict physical harm to anyone who caused offence. Initially the size of a python, it had gradually shrunk, while retaining its strength. To confirm the tale, Ayoh-ha related how once the family was lunching in the foyer when they were startled by a loud crash. They could not determine the cause until a little snake glided up to them. Although the story sounded somewhat ridiculous, Ayoh-ha's fantastical accounts only deepened the murky chasm into which I was falling. Only if I let my rational self go without a struggle could I hope to reconcile with this world of superstition.

Weeks later, the ginger cat was playing in front of my room with what looked like a long earthworm. The thing moved with such quick twitches that arouse my curiosity. When I came closer I realised that it was actually a tiny green snake that lashed from side to side, trying to escape from the cat's claws. My immediate reaction was to shove the cat off, fearing it would kill its new toy. As soon as the reptile broke loose, it slithered away fast and, before I knew it, it slipped through the wall slats of my room. I rushed inside, but it was impossible to find it.

I knew very little about snakes but had bad memories of them. The closest I had been to one was when I was a kid, during my visit to a terrarium that exhibited the world's most poisonous serpents and which ended abruptly when I fainted at the sight of gangrene and amputations while watching a documentary. When I told Ayoh-ha and Faridah of the small incident, they responded with a smile, pleased that the jinn had conceded to show himself to me. Their joy failed to assuage my concern that the parents of this little snake, which was likely a venomous viper, would find their way into my bedroom looking for their lost offspring.

Despite my scepticism, I could not ignore the deep respect and faith professed by those who solicited the *bomoh*'s supernatural abilities. People from all over the region and even from Malaysia turned to him for help. Young men knelt and bowed before him, calling their greetings by grasping his hand with the utmost respect. Not all revered him though The neighborhood was, of course, aware of Ayoh-ha's sacrilegious practices, rites of Hindu origins lost in time immemorial that devotees dismissed as a sinful deviation of the authentic Islamic faith. Many of those pious detractors, however, ended up commending themselves in secret to the supposed blasphemies of a *bomoh* whenever it was that their prayers didn't seem to be heard by The Almighty.

I was privileged to witness how Ayoh-ha performed healing sessions, some on acquaintances, but mostly for those who had been recommended by word of mouth. They brought a wide variety of ailments and afflictions, which ranged from the mundane to the spiritual: drug addiction, injuries, illnesses, failed love affairs, disharmonies of the soul, ghost possessions and curses.

Sometimes Faridah announced we were expecting visitors, but more often than not I just chanced upon them. Varying from two or three to larger groups – once I counted 15 – they were not told about me and I was never formally introduced. This caused some odd situations when villagers found themselves confronted with a Westerner and, most likely, an infidel. They would usually pause speechless, staring at this white man in a sarong, perhaps wondering if I was a vision. The awkward silence would last until someone, often me, dared to utter "Assalamualaikum[12]". After this greeting, they probably assumed I was a Muslim but

---

12 Common greeting in Arabic among Muslims that translates to "Peace be upon you". The appropriate response is "Waalaikumussalam" (And upon you be peace).

refrained from inquiring further until Ayoh-ha would tell them I was a photographer and a good friend of the family. Frequently, they were amazed to learn that I was not visiting, but actually living there.

Malay was the only language spoken, and seeing the foreign features of these women and men, often of Persian or Arab ancestry, Thai felt very foreign. I had heard that within the family, particularly in villages, some parents frowned upon Thai being spoken at home, so my concern was that by using this language I was raising a barrier. However, I never sensed any unease when they replied to me. On the contrary, they remarked how well I spoke it – not that I did – putting my concerns at rest, even though it might be out of politeness. With time, I felt more comfortable whenever we had visitors, and I began to show respect and sincerity by greeting the men in the local Muslim way, clasping both their hands, then bringing my right hand over my heart.

Ayoh-ha performed his healings and exorcisms in different rooms, depending on the number of people involved and the choice of treatment. The process was always preluded with the *bomoh* chatting and even joking with his clients, followed by a series of diagnostic questions. They all came hoping their conditions would be healed or at least alleviated: aging wives that wanted to hold on to husbands who were off with their mistresses; a father with his 15-year-old son who had stolen from his parents to buy drugs; a group of villagers grieving for relatives who had been in prison for months waiting for trial; a man who could hardly walk after being shot in the leg; or a pretty maiden stalked by a lustful male spirit. The rituals involved the use of the four elements, represented by jasmine rice, pond water, forceful, long exhalations and sandalwood burning in a censer. Although I understood neither the conversations nor the meaning of the rituals, I settled myself with propriety among these men and women as merely a witness. During the process, words felt irrelevant, replaced by the subtleties I could read from their eyes, faces, hands, stances and the tone of their voices, be it hope or despair, acceptance or regret, courage or fear. It was as if the recesses of their souls could only be fully revealed here, at the Rumoh Rajo.

Among the visitors, those with whom I became acquainted were a middle-aged couple from a hamlet in the Sungai Golok border district. The husband carried his wife in his arms from their car into the house. Her name was also Faridah. A motorcycle accident had left her crippled, her leg severely wasted and rigid because the knee was so mangled that it could hardly flex. Since hospital treatment had made no progress, the couple had put their faith in Ayoh-ha, in spite of his initial reluctance to treat her because he considered himself insufficiently skilled for her particular case. The *bomoh* claimed that the accident was irrelevant and that she was, in fact, harbouring an evil ghost.

Sometimes the couple came in the late evening, not leaving until past midnight or even just after dawn. Ayoh-ha spent countless hours with her performing rituals and using manipulation and therapeutic massages with herbal ointments prepared by Faridah. During these long sessions, I watched as her face often creased in pain. Her husband wouldn't leave her for a moment, always mindful of every reaction in her body. Sometimes the *bomoh* would pause, absorbed as though he was visualising the bones and joints, trying to comprehend how they worked before proceeding. Although unconvinced by his methods, I admired what I felt was sincere dedication and perseverance. What touched me most was the hope shown by the couple and their blind trust in Ayoh-ha's skills. After weeks of treatment, although she could stretch a bit more than before, she was far from recovered. I felt very sorry for her, as I doubted she would ever walk again without crutches.

* * *

Soon, the only compelling reason to ride into downtown was to meet Hannan. We usually met at Ju's stall to talk over tea and roti, keen to share snippets of my conversations with the family and his latest findings on the Rumoh Rajo. Many of those chats ended with the same question, "Who is Ayoh-ha?" For a start, that was not his real name. "Ayoh" was a proper form of address to elders in Malay and "ha" a contraction of his first name – which we never managed to find out. Faridah alleged that his grandfather had served the supposed Raja, a claim that would grant him certain legitimacy in the house. But if it was so, why had he suddenly left Narathiwat in his youth and where did he go during those 30 years of absence? My attempts to clarify this with him, his mother or Faridah always ended diluted behind a cloud of contradictions and new question marks. And when I tried to find answers to those new questions, more questions arose. Layer after layer, the figure of Ayoh-ha was becoming such a riddle that we chose it to put it aside for the time being and focus on the house.

The last enquiries on the Rumoh Rajo didn't seem to yield results either. Hannan and Pu had twice been to the John F. Kennedy Library[13] at their former college, the Prince of Songkhla University (PSU) in Pattani, to search through documents from local researchers. All they found were history books written in Thai and Malay that they borrowed to write a run-through for me. In them, there was not a single clue that could be remotely related to the house. They would have to look somewhere else, although they were running out of resources.

Then luck took a turn. When they went back to the library to return the books, Pu decided to give it another try and accessed the computer database one last time. Chance took her across a 10-year-old thesis titled, "The Architecture of the Governors' Palaces in the Seven Towns of Pattani". Hannan looked at the last page, expecting to find in the acknowledgments the name of his former art teacher, but there was no mention of Zakariya to be found. The document was in Thai and had a summary in English that explained how the Kingdom of Patani, as the result of four wars and uprisings against Siam, was carved up into seven principalities in the early 19th century. A hundred years later, Siam annexed the region under royal edict and turned it into provinces.

---

13 John F. Kennedy Library is an 8,100 sqm three-storey building located on the PSU campus. It was officially opened in 1973 as an initiative of Colonel Thanat Khoman, the first University president and a committee member of the John F. Kennedy Foundation in Thailand who gave a grant for its construction.

Narathiwat, whose capital was by then called Bang Nara, was one of them. The thesis was devoted to the palaces that once belonged to the Rajas who ruled the Seven Malay Principalities.

In the introduction, a map located the palaces in the geographical area that today comprises the provinces of Yala, Pattani and Narathiwat. Every chapter examined each one of the palaces with architectural descriptions, photographs of interiors and exteriors, and a floor plan. Since the document was a photocopy of the original, images appeared dark and blotted, making it difficult to discern fine details, but in the chapter referred in the thesis as the "Palace of Rangae", I thought I recognised parts of the house.

The distinct features of the floor plan, which matched the spaces so familiar to me, left no room for doubt. It was the Rumoh Rajo. The building was described as being in the "Terengganu style"[14]. In one of the pictures, a copy of what had to be an old photograph, it stood flanked by two more buildings of the same size and features, surely part of the original palace compound. At the end of the chapter appeared a portrait and the name of the last owner and inhabitant: the Raja of Rangae, Tuan Tengku Shamsudeen ("Tuan Tengku" is a Malay royal form of address that could be glossed as "His Highness"). His Siamese title was *Phraya Phupaphakdee Sri Suwan Prathet Wiset Wangsa*, which translated as, "Loyal Lord of the Mountain, Lord of the Golden

---

14 Terengganu is an ancient Malay state that arose in the 6th century and was the first to receive Islam in 1303. It is a constitutive state of present-day federal Malaysia.

Country and Magic Dynasty". Hannan was intrigued by the words "Sri Wangsa", the same dynastic name in Sanskrit as that of the last Raja of Langkasuka who founded the Patani Kingdom in the 14th century. The last page of the document showed a family tree of the Raja's lineage with some names that sounded familiar to me from talks with Ayoh-ha. We were amazed at this find, not least because it coincided with the little that he had told me in fragmentary conversations. I had presumed that his stories were based on local folklore embroidered to impress me. It appeared that we had finally reached solid ground, an opportunity to go beyond the hearsay to unravel the house's foggy past and perhaps uncover the fate of its late owner, the Raja of Rangae, Tuan Tengku Shamsudeen.

* * *

Almost daily, our evenings drew on at Ju's roti stall, immersed in endless chats over Patani's history and its legendary rajas. Hannan told me about a temple that secretly housed the last of the golden trees that Malay rajas sent as triennial tribute to the king of Siam. Unfortunately, access to the artefact by non-Buddhists was restricted, probably due to the political weight that it carried. Another piece of news was a visit to his fellow teacher, who had a wealth of antique photographs from the turn of the twentieth century. One of them that hung in his studio showed a man in white uniform and peaked cap in front of a tiled-roof building. It turned out that his colleague's grandfather was the first Siamese official to take up a post as police chief in the old Bang Nara. This treasury of images needed to be recorded. On the spur of the moment, Hannan took his camera and proceeded to capture them. This upset his colleague, who demanded he erase all the pictures. It did not take much guesswork to realise why he preferred to keep his family's past private, as the one-time chief had been in service during that tempestuous transition between the annexation of the principalities and their merger into the new administrative division of Siam. At some point, Hannan began to lower his voice and throw a few sidelong glances. Something seemed to prick him. Leaning towards me over the table, he whispered, "Shall we talk at my place?" Something odd was going on that I could not follow, but I nodded anyway, and he asked right away for the bill. My friend explained later in the privacy of his home, this time over homemade *teh susu* and sweets served by his wife.

"Did you notice the man sitting alone next to us?" referring to one of Ju's friends, a local who like Ju was in the volunteer rescue corps.

"You mean that big guy with the yellow vest? Yes, I did. Ju once introduced him to me."

"I don't feel comfortable with him around," Hannan said.

"What's wrong with the guy?"

"Have you noticed he always hangs out there and often alone? I think he goes there to watch and listen."

I couldn't help but agree with him. In fact, I, too, had sensed something strange about the man. On one occasion, after asking me to try out my camera, he pulled out a bullet and placed it on the table to get a close up shot. It was usual for civilians – mostly for the Buddhists – to carry guns, but there was something in the bearing of this guy that made me feel a bit uneasy.

Hannan took a sip of tea and concluded, "I have long suspected that he might be a spy."

This took me by surprise and at first I thought he was joking. I recalled what a friend in Pattani had said about informants who worked with the military, mingling with the population. Behind the innocent façade of an ice-cream peddler or a schoolteacher could hide a spy lying in wait to worm information out of children about their families. One negative report was enough for the occupiers to arrest a suspect, often bursting into their homes in the dead of night, without proof of any wrongdoing. Under martial law, in tandem with the emergency decree, a suspect could be held for weeks at any location, usually a military base, without their family being informed. Some never made it home. Just as all this began to sink in, the matter felt too serious to joke about. Then, Hannan dropped the bombshell.

"Some people think that you might be a spy too."

He said this with a broad smile and I began to laugh at the absurdity of such a notion. I suppose I should have realised that as virtually the only Westerner in town my presence was likely to stir the imagination of the locals, particularly the Malay-Muslims.

"Really, and what do you think?" I asked in a sarcastic tone.

Hannan crossed his arms behind his head and leaned back in the chair, delaying his answer while studying me. He seemed to be savouring how the conversation had shifted.

"Well... I am still trying to figure out what exactly you are doing here."

Despite his warm smile, I knew he was serious and I was alarmed by his response, although I tried not to show it. Here was someone who had invited me into his home, treated me as a friend and helped me to find answers, yet nevertheless harboured serious doubts about me. This contradiction made me realise I had failed to understand how I was perceived. A Western foreigner spending a long time in a restive region occupied by the army under martial law was expected to be a journalist, researcher or teacher, but I was none of those. My inability to explain what exactly I was doing in the Deep South, the indefinite nature of my work and my eagerness and curiosity, could well be misinterpreted or even arouse suspicion in a part of Thailand where nothing was quite as it seemed. If even Hannan, who was sympathetic to me, still had a degree of wariness, what might other locals who didn't know me at all be thinking? How could I convince them of my intentions, when I myself was not clear as to my motives for delving into the house's history? However, as far as Hannan was concerned, I realised I could only win his trust once he fully understood the deep impression the house had made on me. Bearing this in mind, I decided it was time to take him there.

Twelve years had passed since Hannan had last seen the house and when he now stood before the ancient palace of the last Raja who had paid tribute to Siam, his heart sank. The state of ruin and disrepair had come about so fast, he told me. In the intervening years, the cancer of neglect had spread through the whole left wing, now partly collapsed, while other parts were going the same way. Reaching the porch, he pointed above the arched doorway, where once there stood a fanlight magnificently carved in Arabic calligraphy with the word of God and a poem to the moon, now usurped by a piece of corrugated scrap metal.

Faridah received us warmly and took us to see Ayoh-ha. He was sitting with Beraheng in the back of the foyer, leaning on the crooked balustrade and absorbed in cutting palm leaf into cigarette-length segments with machine-like precision, while sipping coffee made from his favoured three-in-one mix sachets from 7-Eleven. Next to him was a brass bowl filled with uncooked white rice, his rings buried inside, along with lumps of wood and a flask containing an auburn liquid, by all accounts some sort of incantation in the works.

Hannan knelt down to exchange greetings. The contact of Ayoh-ha's hands sent a stir deep to his bones. This was not an ordinary man, he could tell. We sat down on the mat and Faridah brought a tray with two cups of coffee. The conversation between Ayoh-ha and Hannan, revealed that they were distantly related, which did not surprise me, as everyone around the town seemed to be family in one way or another. Feeling at ease, my friend began to ask about the building without further delay. Some of the answers confirmed what we had already discovered, while others were contradictory. The shaman enjoyed rambling on, telling us local legends and recalling personal anecdotes. A single question would spark an endless 'answer', which mutated into a hallucinatory torrent of tales that had nothing to do with the original query, but nevertheless kept us enthralled.

Awe Sado was a famous outlaw and a magic man. His hideout was located in a cave in Phipit Mountain. It was said that bullets wouldn't harm him. One day, policemen managed to capture the elusive man and proceeded to execute him right away. But he wouldn't die. They tried everything, shooting through his "five doors": mouth, nose, ears, eyes and anus. But he was able to spit bullets out of his mouth. They tried to bury him up to his neck. But after several days without food and water he was still alive.

Awe's younger brother arrived. Taking pity on his elder brother he said that he would help him die. But he feared he did not have enough power to do so. Nevertheless, he tried to put Awe out of his misery by pouring liquid metal into his mouth and down his throat until his heart stopped. Even then, he claimed Awe was still alive.

The policemen transported the corpse to a Muslim cemetery and buried it there. Guards remained on site, lest the deceased was able to rise up again. At three in the afternoon a storm descended on the cemetery. It was not the rainy season, but it poured long and hard. Soon after the rain abated, a huge centipede crawled up from the grave, frightening the guards, who had curled up under a tarpaulin and grown drowsy. Before the centipede could make its getaway, the guards catapulted themselves onto the heinous invertebrate. They almost broke their arms smashing the creature with the butt of their rifles.

Awe Sado's younger brother came to see what had happened

and proclaimed: "Now he is indeed dead." What was left of the centipede was put in a bottle and taken to the cave where the outlaw used to hide.

We had no idea what to make out of the story, unable to see any linkage with the house, but it did not matter. When the *bomoh* narrated these stories, they were no longer folk tales told by a man. In the world of the Rumoh Rajo, this was a truthful account that percolated through the bowels of the house and we were delighted to listen.

Before leaving, Hannan dared to inquire after the panels and for once Ayoh-ha gave a straightforward answer. He said they had been stolen and then sold to an antiquarian for less than 10,000 baht (US$325). He knew this because he had once unsuccessfully tried to retrieve them from the buyer. Named Beloh, he had an antique shop in town.

* * *

Taking our cue from Ayoh-ha, Hannan and I decided to seek out this Mr. Beloh. We had already agreed we should approach him with discretion, careful not to jump to any conclusions and offend him before learning how the panels had ended up in his hands. The antique shop was not hard to find, being near the town centre on the road to Narathat beach. A humble place, it was lined with glass shelves and cabinets where old swords, daggers and knives were displayed on stands. Scattered on the ground lay a muddle of terracotta jars, Chinese porcelain, gongs, miniature sailboats, spears, coins, teapots, brass plates and ceremonial silverware. At the far end, in the shadows, a bald man sat at his desk, bare-chested on account of the heat, his withered and blotchy skin an antique map draped over his body. My first thought was that his features were neither Thai nor Malay but rather Middle Eastern. In fact, after exchanging greetings, Mr. Beloh told us that his father had emigrated from Kashmir. As we shook hands, he grinned with contentment, clearly pleased to see a presumably wealthy foreigner and a potential buyer. I was about to carry on the conversation when Hannan signaled to me to let him deal with the antiquarian, who probably assumed that my companion was there as a mere translator. I stood back, allowing them to speak in Malay. Hannan broke the ice with flattery, saying that I had heard that his establishment was one of the finest in the country and that I was interested in kris, the Malay dagger.

"I see. Is he here to buy one?" Beloh said, darting his eyes up at me.

"If you don't mind, he would like to know first about Malay culture. So before talking business, could you show him some of the best antiques you have?"

Pretending to ignore their conversation, I ran my eyes over a sword of Arab appearance on one of the shelves. On its blade was engraved "1785", the year of an epic war between Siam and Patani. Had this sword been fleshed in that last battle which sealed the demise of the Malay kingdom?

"My friend would like to see special pieces," Hannan added, and immediately Beloh seemed even more interested in me.

"Where are you from and what are you doing in Narathiwat?" he asked me. Then, "Where are you staying?" I guessed that this last question was to establish my financial status. Hannan answered for me:

"He's staying at the Rumoh Rajo Legeh." This response caught him off guard. For a moment he looked flustered, but then it was his turn to surprise us.

"Oh really?" he said, trying to sound indifferent, but we knew he was clearly intrigued.

"Well, I happen to have a kris that belonged to the Raja of Legeh himself."

Hannan turned to me with a triumphant smile. Beloh took a key from his drawer and left the table to unlock one of the sliding glass doors to the wall shelves. From one of these, he removed a kris, carefully drew it out of its wooden sheath and then laid it on the table. Hannan held his breath. This was a relic not only of beauty but also with an arresting presence. The head of some chimerical creature, a hybrid between a bird and a snake, shaped the ivory hilt with a tapering nose bulging forward and curled at its end. From its long neck emerged a sinuous blade with four fingerprint-like marks cast on the igneous metal with bare hands by its maker – a rite to endow the kris with supernatural powers on behalf of the person for whom it was forged.

"I don't believe in that nonsense. I am a businessman, you see? A dagger is a dagger. Anything else is a silly tale for children."

He pointed at the glass shelves flashing a grin.

"Do you see all that collection of mine? Together it is worth

Morning haze over the Bang Nara River with Bukit Tanjong in the background. View from the barbed-wire-protected promenade in Narathiwat town.

The finial crowning the apex of the central front gable on the Rumoh Rajo. Carved with a design inherited from Langkasuka, in a shape that evokes the silhouette of Shiva sitting in meditation and a lotus bud engraved on it.

Waesuraini sits in the attic of the Rumo Rajo, where Shamsudeen died. The entire structure was built without nails, using ancient post-and-beam methods from traditional Malay architecture.

Faridah

Fatimah

Hannan listens to one of Ayoh-ha's stories.

Montree adjusts his sarong before the entrance doorway to the Rumoh Rajo. The arch on top, or *gunungan*, is a symbolic legacy of Mount Meru, the gateway between the other world and ours.

Ayoh-ha performs a late-night ritual on soil from Sisakorn.

Faridah prepares puffed rice to feed the spirits she says dwell in the attic.

Ayoh-ha performs a healing ritual on a teenager to cure him of his drug addiction.

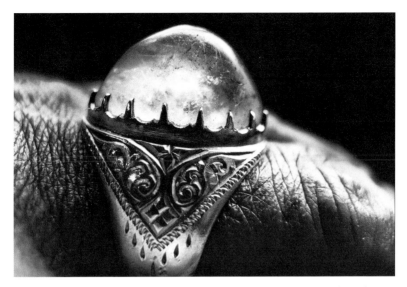

A close-up of one of Ayoh-ha's rings, which he claims are endowed with supernatural powers.

Ayoh-ha shows me his collection of kris, ceremonial Malay daggers.

The only known portrait of Tuan Tengku Shamsudeen, the Raja of Legeh.

The only surviving seal of the Raja of Legeh. Carved in ivory, the script in the centre is Jawi, adapted from the Arabic alphabet to write Malay language in Patani and elsewhere in Malaysia.

The mausoleum of Tuan Tengku Shamsudeen. Old central mosque, Narathiwat town.

The kris that once belonged to Tuan Tengku Shamsudeen.

Heirlooms of a wealthy Siamese family in Narathiwat.

Woodcarving on a wall ventilation panel salvaged from the former
Palace of the Raja of Legeh.

A gift from King Chulalongkorn to Tuan Tengku Shamsudeen.
Collection housed at Khun Laharn Museum, Yingo.

Hannan displays his collection of wooden moulds for ceremonial
cakes, reserved for the sole indulgence of Rajas, a Malay tradition
that only existed in Patani and Kelantan.

Montree holds a finial that fell from the roof.

The *babo* (headmaster) of a school where the victim of a bombing taught, pours water on the burial mound after the funeral prayers.

A soldier waits next to the house while an officer inspects its interior.

Nor, the alleged descendant of Sahmsudeen. Behind her is one of the wooden panels salvaged from the former palace of the Rajas of Legeh that once stood in Tanjong Mas.

36 million! Yes, you heard it right, 36! That is what I am expecting a museum to pay, and when that happens, I will retire."

Hannan looked a little discomposed. For him, a kris was not only the quintessence of his culture, but a precious talisman deeply connected to one's heart and soul, something that embodies who you are, your life. For the Thai authorities, on the other hand, a kris was nothing but a war weapon and years ago a ban on kris-making and their possession was enforced throughout the three troubled provinces. Now kris lay piled up in markets like useless props or collectibles at best. Only those who truly treasure them have secretly kept them in the family as heirlooms.

Hannan asked permission to hold the kris. The line of its hand-wrought blade was sinuous and elegant, with a damascene-like texture that felt organic as if wood had blended with stone. We stood staring at it for a while. Then Hannan brought it close to smell its scent.

Pleased to see how impressed we were, Beloh showed us other kris from his collection. While we admired them he asked Hannan casually, "And what does he do in the Rumoh Rajo?"

Hannan replied that I was an artist interested in the history of Southern Thailand, and then, without warning, he pulled from his case the prints of the wooden panels, explaining that I was looking for these particular pieces and that this is why I was there. Beloh was unable to conceal his surprise but he was not forthcoming about their whereabouts. He stared at the photos for some time before saying, "Well, I can try to find out about them if he is really interested," implying that either he had them or he knew who did. Hannan asked him to estimate the price of a single piece, but Beloh would not be drawn. If there was to be a sale, he told us it should include the complete set of 26 pieces (he knew the exact number) at a rough price of 200,000 baht. The precise sum could be agreed upon eventually, he added.

(As a postscript, two years later, Hannan would see the panels on display at the Khun Laharn local museum in Yingo whose owner had purchased them from Beloh.)

It was nearly seven in the evening. The last prayer of the day would soon be called and Beloh seemed reluctant for us to stay much longer. But then unexpectedly he said, "Before you leave I have something very special to show you."

Shuffling away, he returned carrying a wad of keys. With one of them, he opened a drawer from his table and removed a small lacquered wooden casket. He jangled again through the keys and pulled another one to open it. Inside was a small round object. Beloh let Hannan inspect it. It was a seal made of elephant ivory, with a teardrop-shaped symbol embossed on one side and the bottom engraved with a circular pattern in the centre of which were inscriptions in Jawi[15], the Arabic script used to write Malay.

"Where did it come from?" Hannan asked, intrigued.

"From the Rumoh Rajo."

---

15 Jawi is an Arabic script used to write the classical Malay language that replaced the Indian script due to the spread of Islam in Southeast Asia from the 14th century. Dutch and British colonialism led to the demise of Jawi, which was gradually replaced during the 19th century by a Latin script called Rumi, currently official in Malay-speaking countries. Today, Jawi is still used in Thailand's Deep South as everyday writing by elders and is taught in private schools.

Hannan's eyes lit up and he asked the price.

"It is not for sale," said the antiquarian, retrieving the seal from Hannan's hand and concluding, "You may see this only once. Never again."

I quickly asked permission to take a picture. We could hear the last prayer being called and Beloh told us that he was closing his shop.

We came away with many questions left unanswered and could not understand why Beloh was so zealously guarding the seal. Hungry for answers, we rushed back to Hannan's house where we closely examined the photograph I had taken. The image had to be inverted and enlarged on the computer for Hannan to decipher the carved inscription. It read: *Negeri Kuala Menara Salam Legeh*. (Menara state port of peace Legeh.) 'Menara' means 'tower' in Malay and 'Legeh' coincided with the name mentioned several times by Ayoh-ha. There were also the numbers 0001 and 310 carved in Arabic. Feeling this seal was a notable relic, the following weekend Hannan consulted a historian and lecturer at PSU, in the hope that he could elucidate the inscription's meaning. The historian raised his eyebrows, unaware that the seal existed. He confirmed Hannan's translation and explained about 'Legeh', the name whose meaning was so elusive to us.

After Siam annexed the region at the beginning of the 20th century, the Malays of the extinct Kingdom of Patani saw their identity as destined to perish. Many vernacular Malay cities and towns were renamed using Thai nomenclature. Thus, Singgora – the City of Lions – was renamed "Songkhla", a word with no meaning. The same happened to "Rangae", the name of the palace we had found in the thesis, which was actually a corruption of Legeh, the original title of the Raja. Legeh, had been called in its earliest form Langueh, a polity forming part of the Hindu kingdom of Langkasuka and later one of the 13 states that comprised the Kingdom of Patani. Today, the name of Legeh is only vaguely echoed in its ill-fated eponym, Rangae, a Red Zone district of Narathiwat province. The historian surmised that, judging by the yellow and red colouration of the ivory, the seal was more than 200 years old and the engraved numbers signified that at that time the Legeh dynasty had been ruling for 310 years.

A unique keepsake of a broken past, the seal provided tangible evidence for the existence of an obscure lineage of Rajas that, despite having been one of the earliest dynasties in Southeast Asia, disappeared from the pages of history, buried under those who emerged victors and whose memories faded in its sole memorial – the House of the Raja.

* * *

At the end of May, Fatimah announced that she was going to move to a village in Yingo, a more convenient location for her husband and her children, who would be enrolled in a *ponoh* (private Islamic school) nearby. She asked me to visit them whenever I could. Faridah arranged a farewell ceremony with dishes that included turmeric sticky rice, grilled chicken and assorted fruits, the whole adorned with flowers of seven colours.

Ayoh-ha pronounced Allah's blessing for the family in the next stage of their life's journey. It felt that this was the right time to bid my farewell to the house. I needed space and time away to assimilate all I had seen and learned. My departure this time felt very different, as if leaving behind not just friends but family. Yet, I was not sad and when the plane landed at Suvarnabhumi Airport in Bangkok, everything I had experienced in the Deep South remained with me.

A good opportunity soon arose to share my work about the house when H. Ernest Lee, the owner of H Gallery in Bangkok, wanted to hold an exhibition of my photographs. We discussed the title, in the end deciding on the English translation of its vernacular, "The House of the Raja". The exhibition took place at the end of the hot season and I invited Hannan and Pu to the opening reception. I was proud to have them there, as they were part of what I treasured the most in Narathiwat. Although shy and unused to this sort of event, I knew they were excited and enjoyed themselves. Hannan was now able to grasp the meaning behind the photographs and as he and his wife left the gallery he told me with his beaming smile, "Now I understand."

The exhibition could have marked an end to my journeys in the Deep South, but questions lingered. H., who knew my obsession's corrosive power, urged me to move on from the house and expend my energy in a new direction. But I could not. And it would not be long before I submitted to the compelling force calling me back to the House of the Raja.

STORMS OVER
LEGEH

～III～

With the onset of the rainy season, the night's shadows refused to submit to the dawn. The sun was held captive behind towering clouds, tenebrous men-of-war gliding in from the ocean seeking to besiege Narathiwat.

The barrage of rain could last for days without pause, causing severe floods in town. A deluge splashed down onto the gables, water creeping its way through the countless fissures, hollows and pits of the house, drenching large parts of the wooden floors and causing stains that spread like a pernicious disease. Rainwater saturated the beams and rafters, dripping slowly to the ground in dark amber globs, as if the house's lifeblood was draining away. Squalls battered the shutters against the façade with such violence that we had to keep them closed, and we sheltered in the shadows of the interior, that became sombre and damp. During such moments, it felt as if Mother Nature was reclaiming the wood and the stone, threatening to swallow the house with her raging force, leaving no trace that the building had ever existed. The house became a wildlife haven. Feral cats roamed inside at will and brawled with each other. In the evenings, the odd bat flapped over my head and the dampness brought more mosquitoes than ever. All sorts of insects crawled into my room and rubbing ants off my sleeping mat became a nightly routine. Even cockroaches made my camera bag their temporary home. An outsider might conclude that the gloomy atmosphere made my stay harder. Yet, despite these annoyances, I felt in a state of bliss as if I were finally at peace with the House of the Raja.

Fatimah lived with her children in Yingo district. Pantawong and Waesuraini were left under her care to be schooled there and the sisters' father was back in his village. Only Ayoh-ha and Faridah stayed. Without the children playing around, the mood in the house was lonely and quiet. On one occasion, two Malaysian women who had caught sight of the building from the road while driving down to the border ventured inside presuming it abandoned. When they appeared in the courtyard, they were taken aback to find a Westerner in undies. Fortunately, one of them spoke English well enough so I could explain myself. I called Faridah over to receive them and this she did warmly, holding their hands lovingly as if the two strangers were her own sisters. One of them asked permission to take a look at the attic and after she did, came down flustered saying that she had felt some sort of presence up there.

Unrelenting days of rain meant fewer visitors. The husband and his crippled wife, whom Ayoh-ha had been treating so persistently for months, were among the few who visited. The last time I had seen the couple, the husband still had to carry his wife in his arms from their car into the house. Her knee had an increased range of motion, but it was still far from a complete recovery. Now I barely recognised the new person in front of me. The sadness in her eyes, the grimace of pain across her face and the air of gloom surrounding her had gone. Looking radiant and full of life, with a few extra kilos, she walked without the slightest limp as if nothing had ever happened to her leg. I could not believe my eyes. The happy couple laughed at my look of incredulity. I had been certain that her condition would not improve further, no matter how strong their faith or how much time and effort Ayoh-ha invested in his curative incantations. Confronted by the evidence, I suspended my disbelief about Ayoh-ha's powers. Whatever therapeutic skills he might have, it was hard to believe they could yield such incredible results and I began to wonder whether he indeed possessed sanative faculties that escaped rational explanation.

Ayoh-ha never tried to prove his so-called powers to me and I always concealed my scepticism from him out of deference. I had also understood that, in spite of my scientific and rational education, there was little to be gained from questioning this hinterland of superstition in which I had decided to immerse myself. This brought me to the irony of inhibiting my judgment as to the most lucid choice. Now, I began to find myself willing not to subdue reason, but to abandon it all together and surrender to the call of the arcane world in which Faridah and Ayoh-ha lived. It was as if, betrayed by my own will, the left hemisphere of my brain, the side of logic and linear thinking, was being superseded by the one in which imagination and dreams hold sway.

*　*　*

Waking in the middle of the night to deafening thunderstorms and the hammering of rain on the roof, I glance around me through the wispy veil of the mosquito net. My room flickers, turned into a fragile wooden box. Outside in the courtyard, the water pouring on the ground produces a deep, rhythmic resonance, trying to penetrate my consciousness. The sound feels familiar, somehow connected with the water in my body. "Water with water." I close my eyes, trying to ignore this strange thought. Instead, the sound of the rain begins to acquire a more specific dimension inside my mind. The vast mass, plunging down restlessly like a waterfall, starts to split into infinite layers, a stream of anonymous voices whispering in unknown languages. I seem to feel the burst of every single drop among billions smashing against the surface of the house. After a while, the deafening sound subsides and, as the rain abates, a second noise arises, a symphony of frogs echoing through the dark. Then the rain redoubled strength as if trying to defeat the frogs' frenzy and the amphibian mantra slowly surrenders. My consciousness is trying to unravel the rustle. Voices of ages past. The more I try to sleep, the more futile my efforts are.

* * *

Faridah awakes before dawn. She washes her face and limbs with fresh water from the well in the courtyard. She then dons her embroidered magnolia white prayer robes and steps gently onto a red-patterned carpet. As she kneels down, swaying her arms forward, her robes billow out like a wing outspread in the shadows until she falls prostrate, her white figure a marble statue. The early morning breeze pauses at the interval between darkness and light. Her pale figure rises and falls.

Silence...

She slowly arises from the shadows. Standing in front of the window, through which the dawn's first glimmer spills, she brings her palms over her face. Light gilds her skin at the end of her prayer. Faridah folds her garment neatly, places it on the carpet and rests quietly in a dry corner of the foyer.

The clouds grant a rare lull. The alchemy of morning turns everything into gold, briefly secreted in the mist that extends its feathery fingers over the riverbanks. Presently, everything around the house has disappeared. Faridah stares wistfully at the coconut trees whose tops soar like the wings of a garuda over the white froth. She mumbles something and I see a light radiating from her dark eyes. Turning to me with a flicker of a smile, she repeats what I could not hear a moment ago, "I miss Sisakorn."

Faridah missed the tough but happy times of her childhood in the jungles of her village, the sounds with which she grew up, the afternoon baths at the waterfall pools with her family after rubber tapping, the fire's warmth when nights cooled during the rainy season and, most of all, the air of freedom that caressed her when she ran barefoot through the lush rainforest.

In the early 1970s, the rugged mountains of the remote district secured the hideouts of communist guerrillas, who often came down from the hills to request supplies from villagers who had no choice but to comply. The jungle also harboured smaller bands of separatist insurgents who had sprung from local communities and were empathetic and helpful to villagers during hard times. Her family lived in a secluded wood cabin within easy reach of their orchard and rubber plantation, accessed only by a forest trail trodden by humans and animals. In those times villagers often arranged hunting parties to kill intruding beasts.

From the very moment of her birth, Faridah revealed herself as a girl out of the ordinary. She departed her mother's womb inside the amniotic sac, a creature arrived from another world in the gaping eyes of those present. When they ripped apart the tissue to retrieve the newborn, a coronet of flowers of seven different colours garnered her hair, only to disappear in a moment. A murmur of astonishment and prayers filled the tiny candle-lit room where the natural birth had taken place.

Despite the initial dismay, everything seemed normal in this baby girl until the age of three. It was then that she refused to eat anything that was not puffed rice, the sacred aliment with which shamans nourished their spirits since Vedic times and what would be her exclusive diet until she turned seven. At that age, the girl seemed to return to a normal state.

Before dawn, Faridah used to accompany her mother to sell their fruits and vegetables at the morning market in Kampung Kalong. Sometimes, her little sister Fatimah would follow them unseen, playing hide and seek behind trees and shrubs until she was caught and scolded by her mother, who ordered Faridah to escort her naughty sister home. The trek took hours through waning vestiges of fog, over hills and across plantations and a pristine creek where encounters with herds of wild elephants or panthers were not uncommon. The forest never frightened Faridah but rather kindled in her a sense of belonging that she could never find in people.

One morning, when her parents were away tapping rubber, she sat under banyan trees playing with Fatimah on her lap. Suddenly, she found herself surrounded by snakes: five pythons that approached carefully and stopped a couple of metres away from her. Their skin and eyes were of a yellow she had never seen before, glowing from within the flesh underneath. She remained calm and smiled at them. The snakes raised their heads from the ground and looked into her eyes, hissing as if expecting a response. Unfazed, she said her name and after asking the pythons not to scare her sister because she was too small, they slithered back into the forest. Since this strange encounter, Faridah talked to the trees, to the tiger roaming around their home at night, to the elephants bathing in the pools of the creek and to the owls watching from the depths of the forest. All seemed to listen to her words and understand what she meant. They became acquainted with her scent and Faridah could recognise theirs.

Faridah responded to the call of her new world, sneaking away from her family to wander alone in the jungle until nightfall. Fireflies always escorted her home, shedding tenuous spangles of light along the way. Several times had her parents to search for her at the untimeliest hours, lantern in hand, fearing something bad had happened to their daughter because of the many dangers that might await deep in those forests, not just beasts that crawled out of their lairs craving for human flesh, but humans themselves who had grown rebellious those days. There was also a group of aboriginals, the last of their kind, who only appeared visible when their spirits of rain drove them down from the mountains where they hid from the rest of the world. But the dread of her parents would suddenly end when they found Faridah maundering and cheerful, and she would show them with great excitement a flower that had bloomed before her eyes and leaves of healing plants she had found, following the voices of invisible cicerones she was convinced guided her. She could be away for an entire day, causing big headaches to her parents who were uncertain whether imagination or insanity thrived in her.

Villagers feared the girl. She wouldn't hesitate to confront whoever dared harm the forest or its inhabitants. Those villagers saw with terror how this little girl's face transmogrified into the semblance of a tiger or a snake.

Those were convulsed times. Rumours had it that separatist insurgents had abducted a wealthy Chinese businessman whilst he was visiting his copper mine in the Rangae district. There were reports that he took his chances, escaping in the confusion of a firefight that broke out when his captors stumbled upon a party of communist guerrillas.

As she would often do before daybreak, Faridah sat by the window, the rest of her family asleep. She liked to contemplate how the forest slowly awoke. Rain had been pouring all night and now was rising back to the sky as a ghostly veil. But that morning, something else loomed from the brume that surrounded the house. At first, she thought it was one of her magical friends who had decided to visit her. Gradually bathed in the dawning light, it became apparent this figure was human. A man. Faridah went outside to receive the stranger. He approached carefully. His forehead gleamed with sweat, his black moustache imposing and the barrel of a gun winking below his raincoat. The girl did not feel any fear. In fact, the presence of the stranger made her feel safe. With a grave and calm voice, he asked for water. She smiled at him, scampered into the house to fetch a bowl and filled it to the brim. The man drank it at a stretch. He thanked her with a smile that made his moustache even bigger and, without sparing a word, turned swiftly and vanished into the bush. Faridah was ten and wondered if she would see him again.

When Faridah reached puberty, her parents thought that the chores of matrimony would do well to their fantasising daughter, so they made arrangements with a suitor from Russo. The marriage ended abruptly three months later, when Faridah absconded from her husband to undertake a long walk back home to Sisakorn. Nothing would persuade her to return to him, obliging her parents to reluctantly reimburse the money received for the dowry.

Three years later, she married again, this time voluntarily, although pressed by her parents. She had a son, Pantawong. At first, her husband proved kind and even exceeded his measure of patience, listening to her encounters with a lady dressed in red and long hair who lived in a tree or with wild elephants that bowed in her presence. But concerned with only worldly and prosaic endeavours, he grew tired of her childish daydreaming and what he called "aspirations to be a wanderer but not a wife".

Far worse problems stem from her third marriage to a soldier who suffered episodes of hostility due to his abuse of kratom[16]. He believed her to be dallying men during the time she spent alone in the forest and often resorted to physical violence as punishment. It was to him Faridah owed the loss of some of her teeth. After this marriage also ended, Faridah vowed not to trust men again. Where other women could gain and grab hold of their happiness, she only found a barren life. Only the natural world and its invisible inhabitants had found a place in her heart.

After listening to her story, I wondered what had taken Faridah from her home. It had to relate to Ayoh-ha. He had told me during one of his reminiscences that he had known her as a child, but did not elaborate. Perhaps she had found in the *bomoh* a kinship with the unseen world that so lovingly had nurtured her in the jungles of Sisakorn. Thus, despite the desolation of the inclement weather and the absence of both her daughter and her son, Faridah remained by Ayoh-ha's side.

---

16 A tropical evergreen tree native to Southeast Asia. The leaves have opiate properties and are chewed to increase energy and sexual desire.

* * *

On dry days, I would make my way downtown to see Hannan and Pu. Pu was an excellent cook and always indulged us with an array of delicious northern and southern dishes. The homemade cooking and the warm and contented feeling of being accepted as a family member kept me away from the tea shops. After the evening meal, Hannan and I would swap our latest findings in conversations that would stretch late into the night.

Hannan's growing reputation as a keen researcher with expertise on local history came to the attention of a university lecturer in Narathiwat who recommended him to the provincial governor's office. He was proposed to join a committee of experts set up to advise on the development of a new cultural museum in town. When the board received the first draft of the official interim dossier, the history of the province appeared riddled with errors and inconsistencies, the worst being the omission of the Kingdom of Patani, whose sultans appeared as mere princelings at the service of the Kingdom of Siam. All the members of the committee, including Hannan, refused to endorse fallacies paraded as history and sent the document back with many corrections. A back and forth between the governor's office and the committee followed, each one as absurd as the next. Frustrated, the scholars resigned one after another with the excuse of being too busy with their full-time jobs. The infinite patience that Hannan possessed took him to be the last one to quit. As he saw it coming, the governor's office appointed a more pliant committee willing to accept the controversial dossier beforehand. The issues did not end here, however.

The Thai government reckoned that, despite the travel advisories issued by other countries, they could turn the troubled province into a celebrated tourist destination. For that purpose, the director of the Tourism Authority in Pattani had a brilliant idea: to put on display the magnificent *Seri Patani*, a massive siege cannon – coat of arms of the provincial flag – that once protected the Patani royal citadel against Siamese invasions. After the destruction of the Malay Kingdom at the end of the 18th century, the cannon was taken as war booty by the Siamese army to Bangkok. Exhibiting the original, today on display in front of the Ministry of Defense in the capital, was out of question, so the fine arts department built a replica that would be sited in front of the remarkable Krue Se Mosque, a 16th-century structure of bricks supported by round pillars and oval arcades that reminded me of medieval cloisters in Spain. The director rubbed her hands together thinking of the crowds of tourists that would flock to see the impressive cannon. She convened a meeting with experts in local culture to hear their opinions, among them Hannan and Baeming. The idea was not well received by everyone. Two years earlier, a general of the Royal Thai Army, descendant of Rajas – his heritage from the only dynasty that came to terms with Siam upon the annexation of Patani and whose former palace is the only one that has made it to this day in mint condition – had conveyed a petition signed by more than a hundred thousand people to the King of Thailand, requesting the return of the cannon. This would surely prove a goodwill gesture conductive of the path towards peace in the Deep South, but the appeal did not meet with a positive response.

A few academics were lukewarm to the proposal from the Tourism Authority. Hannan was appalled. Placing a reproduction of the symbol of defeat of a nation, next to its oldest and holiest mosque, with the purpose of driving the economy of a region whose development budget was in the hands of the military, seemed to Hannan nothing more than a leg-pull and sheer humiliation. He forewarned that, were they to carry out the idea, someone would blow the thing up. The director disregarded what she thought was an overreaction and a few months later, a brand-new replica of the cannon stood in front of Krue Se, awaiting the flood of visitors. It lasted just nine days.

When Hannan received a call from the consternated director, informing that a bomb had split the cannon in two and asking what he had to do with it, he wondered if he was going to be held unfairly liable for damaging public property.

To add insult to injury, the halved remains from the incident revealed that the three million baht (around 90,000 USD) to forge the cannon had been actually spent in a big plumbing pipe painted to simulate antique bronze. Weeks later, the shoddy wreck was sent for repair by the stubborn department of tourism, knowing of the possible consequences.

These edifying events convinced Hannan that taking the initiative with his own projects was a far more productive and rewarding endeavour. Looking for something familiar to start with, he had been to his maternal grandparents' home, an old wooden house whose doors had been locked for years after their death, falling into disrepair. Its deplorable state echoed the decadence of Rumoh Rajo, a sad reminder that what was left of his culture was now in danger.

Inside the house, there were still old personal belongings and antiquities that his mother had considered things worthless. Infected by my same obsession, Hannan deemed anything that belonged to the past of extraordinary value that deserved to be cared for and preserved. He remembered a cabinet, the access to which had been forbidden during his childhood. Inside, he found a linen bag containing a few antiques, among them a brass vase and a white enamel food carrier decorated with colourful flowers. The bag had a tag inscribed with the words "Ini hadiah dari Rajo Legeh" ("This is a gift from the Raja of Legeh"). It was only now that he discovered that these items had actually been a present from Tengku Shamsudeen himself to his maternal grandfather. He would keep this strand of memory as a small treasure.

Hannan's grandfather was a notable *ulama*[17] and astronomer. He had amassed an extensive library of books and documents on astronomy and Islamic studies, as well as an archive of his personal manuscripts written in Jawi and Arabic, garnered over a lifetime during his travels to Mecca and the Middle East. After the death of her parents, Hannan's mother contended that there

---

17 A member of a body of Muslim scholars trained in Islam and Islamic law, who are the interpreters of Islam's sciences and doctrines and laws and the chief guarantors of continuity in the spiritual and intellectual history of the Islamic community.

was not enough space at their home and abandoned the library to its fate. Over the years, rainwater had leaked in and drenched the shelves, ruining most of the books and documents. Termites had devoured the rest. Hannan could only salvage a few pages in Jawi. Now, holding them with great care as if they were rare incunabula, he showed me a journal of algebraic Earth rotation and lunar-phase calculations painstakingly handwritten by his grandfather.

The loss of his family's library was not an isolated case in town. Others perished every year when the tiled roofs of old wooden houses caved in during rainy season. A few weeks later, the oldest bookstore in town – which I remembered to have visited only once because there were no books in English – had closed down upon the death of its owner. The widow found herself with a faltering business she knew little about, so she decided to get rid of it and burn all the books. Hannan, who fortunately was passing by at the time she was flinging the books in the back of a pick-up truck, tried to dissuade her by imploring her to donate them to a library. But the woman refused to listen, asking him rudely to mind his own business. What had once been a beloved haven of knowledge treasured by their late owners went to waste like garbage without anyone seeming to care, a legacy lost through general apathy on the part of the local populace.

The Rumoh Rajo was a silent plea from a languishing heritage that, without custodians, would soon vanish. With this in mind, Hannan had established a group called Pattani Architecture to share and foster the artistic and cultural heritage of a region in the hope of passing his passion on to others. This community was growing into a movement that had attracted the interest of an architect from Songkhla who devised a project to renovate the building and which he wished to propose to the owners.

Hannan had focused his research into the alleged descendants of the Raja based on the names in the thesis, but although he had found out that they lived in Tanjong Mas, he had no means of tracing their exact address. We needed a stroke of luck.

During one of our trips to Pattani, I asked him to stop by a building of traditional design that stood out from other houses in the area. The propietor was a stout Muslim district chief in Yingo called Baeming. Bulky, with hitched breath and a sweaty brow, his face seemed to have frozen in a permanent rictus of bad mood. I could see that he distrusted me. When he learned that I was staying at the Rumo Rajo, Baeming was convinced that behind my façade of a photographer was a treasure hunter seeking a consignment of gold that locals believed had been hidden down a well in Kampung Takok during the Second World War – this he confessed to me weeks later after he proved himself to be wrong.

The owner of a building materials company, Baeming had never been interested in art or history until he came across a museum of Malay artefacts and handicrafts in Kelantan. There, the beauty of mythical creatures and talismanic motifs exquisitely carved in wood, ivory and silver, captivated him in a way he had not felt before. From that day on, he devoted himself to collecting antiques, making the rounds of villages throughout the southern provinces to acquire old items from local families: swords, daggers, old coins, pottery, utensils and even handwritten

Qur'ans. Many of those antiquities were treasured heirlooms that would otherwise have been sold for a pittance to foreign or local buyers for auction to collectors overseas.

Among his most precious works of art was a voluminous album that his father had assembled decades ago in a lifetime of travels through the southern provinces. It was only now that his newborn passion jogged his memory to revisit its forgotten pages; fine coloured drawings of intricate woodcarvings in Langkasuka style copied from traditional timber buildings: stalks, leaves and tendrils that entwined with flower buds, lotus blossoms and cosmic and geometric motifs. None of those carvings exist today, replaced by botched monstrosities of raw concrete. Despite being offered a substantial sum by a curator from a museum in Malaysia who was after the invaluable drawings, Baeming refused to sell.

Around the time I first arrived at the house, Baeming had started constructing a building without knowing its ultimate purpose. With the passing of the months, the construction expanded taking on a life of its own, as if Baeming's subconscious had hatched a plan to build a home for his treasures. His wife and other relatives, not sharing what they regarded as a compulsive obsession for hoarding old things, had initially seen his project as an expensive eccentricity but gradually realised the value of preserving their cultural heritage and appreciated Baeming's determined efforts. When word of his project spread, the villagers began to donate all kinds of antiques and artefacts to his growing museum, now given the name of Khun Laharn. Baeming had also tried, so far unsuccessfully, to acquire the seal of the Raja of Legeh from Beloh, the antiquarian Hannan and I had visited months ago.

During our first visit to his emergent museum, he was thrilled to show us a hunting rifle and a court sword, its guard engraved with celestial motifs and the Chakri Dynasty emblem, originally presented by the Siamese King Rama V to Tuan Tengku Shamsudeen and now donated by the Raja's heirs. It was to take quite a few meetings with Baeming, however, until we gained his trust and he agreed to take us to meet them.

* * *

After waiting at Hannan's home for the downpour to pause, I arrived back past midnight. Crossing the foyer and the central hall, I saw that the doorway to Faridah's room was ajar. It was too late for greetings but hearing a whisper, I tiptoed to the doorway and peeked through the golden curtain that veiled the interior. Inside, the glow of a candle sifted down through the mosquito net upon Ayoh-ha, his shadow trembling and murmuring incantations without taking a breath. Behind him Faridah was asleep. He had not noticed me and, fearing I might disturb him, I decided to turn back. As I crept across the hall to my room, the whispering ceased and the words "Assalamualaikum" echoed behind me. "Waalaikumsalam," I replied immediately, standing motionless for a second, unsure of what to do next.

Then I slowly retraced my steps and drew back the curtain. Ayoh-ha had resumed his recitations. He sat cross-legged on his mat, his bare dark torso swinging back and forth, holding prayer beads in his hands. Without opening his eyes, he beckoned me to enter and join him. He had piled three pillows in front of him to chest height and on top of them there was an open cloth bag whose contents I could not see. I sat in front of him in silence. It was a warm and humid night. Water escaped my body in beads of sweat that mingled with each other in microscopic rivers streaming down my back.

The ritual continued for nearly an hour during which he would occasionally lean over to blow long and hard onto the bag, casting some sort of spell upon its contents. I waited patiently for him to finish and when he did, Ayoh-ha put the prayer beads around his neck, lit a palm-leaf cigarette and puffed away without a word, taking long drags with the same nonchalant air he adopted at the end of all his ceremonies. Snakes of smoke slithered out of his lips and curled up masking his face. The netting dangled over him like a gauzy shroud swaying in the breeze that wafted through the window. Outside, the rain resumed its unrelenting hiss.

Having seen his smug grin, I knew Ayoh-ha was ready to talk so I asked him what was in the bag. He explained it was earth that Faridah's brother had collected from a piece of land in Sisakorn he was interested in buying. Since he needed time to gather the money for the purchase, he had asked Ayoh-ha to use his talents to ensure that the property would not be sold to anyone else. If someone were foolish enough to buy that land, the spell would cause him to suffer swellings in his stomach and extreme pain he told me. It took three hours to create such a spell. This was not the first time he had performed similar ceremonies to ensure land deals in Sisakorn. Hoping that he was in the mood for one of his late-night stories, I seized the opportunity to ask how the sisters had come from Sisakorn to the house. The story he told me had all the makings of one of his fables...

The remote Sisakorn had in the old times been a district rich in gold and copper. Its mines were exhausted long ago, but in its rugged mountains still hid deposits of semiprecious stones highly sought after by Malay shamans. Ayoh-ha's elder son was a gem merchant who often visited the district on business. In a market in the town of Ruso, he met the youngest of the sisters and, after courting for a few months, they married and lived with her family on the same piece of land where they built their house. One day, the entire family fell ill without any apparent reason and the doctor could not offer a medical diagnosis. After several restless nights, Ayoh-ha's son suggested that they should all go to Kampong Takok to be treated by his father.

When the *bomoh* received them in the Rumoh Rajo, he immediately recognised Faridah but said nothing.

After a first examination, he concluded that someone had cast an evil spell on them. He made Faridah bring a basket of salt and told them to sit forming a semicircle in front of him. Then he recited verses from the Qur'an pausing at times to blow on the salt. Next, he threw handfuls over the various members of the family. Immediately, everyone broke into howls of pain so loud that some neighbours rushed over, horrified by the noise and fearful that some kind of assault was taking place. After many nerve-racking minutes their screams subsided, and with them, their aches and pains. They all deemed that the ritual had expelled whatever evil had taken root and the family returned to Sisakorn convinced that all would be well.

However, several days later the same symptoms returned. They asked Ayoh-ha to help them again, this time in Sisakorn, as they felt too weak to travel. When the *bomoh* arrived he took a handful of earth to smell. He then closed his eyes and prayed. Afterwards, he asked them to supply a sackful of salt, over which he blew and recited the same spells as before. He spread the salt around on the land surrounding the two houses and, as he did so, faint whines of anguish began to emerge here and there.

Ayoh-ha went to inspect the spots where the sinister keening came from to find that a variety of items had surfaced: waxed needles, stone amulets, tufts of human hair and cloths soaked in menstrual blood – all objects used in Brahmanic rituals. Ayoh-ha concluded that they had probably been buried by jealous Buddhist neighbours who had hired the talents of a Brahmanic shaman to expel them from the land.

Sadly, despite the successful exorcism, the family misfortunes were still not over.

One evening, Fatimah came to her parents' house crying, soaked through and shuddering in terror. After her mother calmed her down, Fatimah explained that she had gone alone that morning to tap rubber. On her way back home, she met a neighbour at the bridge crossing the stream who suggested catching some fish together. They stood on the riverbank, trying to find a prime spot, when the man suddenly attacked her. After the initial shock, she realised that he was intending to rape her and fought back fiercely. The man retaliated by pounding her stomach repeatedly, pulling her hair and trying to drown her in the river. The fight raged on. He drew a knife and tried to stab her several times but missed. She proved tougher than she looked. Fatimah, knowing that she would not be able to struggle much longer, managed to trick him into believing that someone was approaching. Gathering all her strength, she punched him hard, releasing his grip, and ran up the hill as fast as she could. Then she hid in a gorge. There she waited until dusk, when it felt safe enough to make her way home.

Her parents listened to her story in horror and when they asked her to name the attacker, Fatimah brought her hands to her face and cried. Pulling herself together, she whimpered a name to which her parents reacted in disbelief and disgust. When they went to her sister's house, Faridah did not believe them, but it was the last day she saw her husband. The police tried to track him but, according to rumours, he had fled to Malaysia. From that day on, Fatimah felt unsafe in her own home, even if the doors and windows remained locked. She could hear the attacker banging around, cursing and swearing, trying to break in and finish her off, a nightmare that has haunted her to this day. For months, Fatimah mistrusted men, feeling uncomfortable in the presence of any male other than her husband. Only after numerous healing sessions with a female shaman was her peace of mind restored.

The whole episode caused a commotion in the village and stirred up rumours about Fatimah whose beauty, according to gossip, was tantalising and wicked. Tired of their troubled life, the sisters agreed to Ayoh-ha's advice that they move into the Rumoh Rajo, safe from the nefarious spells and machinations of their home village.

A few days after that strange night, I got the chance for another tête-à-tête with Ayoh-ha. In his typical fashion, he would lean back slightly and straighten himself with great self-confidence. This time, he stooped down and spoke to me of a distant past in a trembling voice, his eyes welling with tears and, at one point, the *bomoh*'s spirit wilted for a moment and I found myself facing a defeated old man. Although I could not always make sense of what he was telling me, I sensed grief and loss in his words, weighed down with resignation, his tales so intriguing that I kept listening quietly, offering the occasional nod. He spoke of wild times, of death, an early release from a 27-year sentence, and made other oblique, fragmented remarks.

"There were many weapons before, AK...do you want it? Take it, I am already old..." and then he would revive, winding up with a sinister note:

"The boys around here know who I am, they know if I say I'll do something, I'll do it for sure. I am not afraid of death, or of anyone. We all die. The entire world will die! I have eyes, you have eyes. I have legs, you have legs. We are the same. I only fear God."

I did not ask him to explain. It would have been pointless, since a chat with Ayoh-ha always included an element of mystery, and I didn't really want to know the truth anyway. I preferred to imagine him many years ago, emerging from the mists of Sisakorn, a fighter, who before the monsoons, prowled down from the hills for supplies, a man who had come across this little girl living with her parents in a jungle cabin; a girl who had a knack for the unseen and to whom he would be bound for the rest of his life.

* * *

Hannan announced with excitement that Baeming would drive us to Tanjong Mas sub-district to visit one of the Raja's descendants. We set out in the morning and headed south, towards the border with Malaysia. On our way, we stopped at a roadside market to buy apples and oranges as a small present, a local protocol we followed with all our visits. We ventured into one of the so-called Red Zones. Despite the presence of a military post at its entrance, the village was ostensibly calm. The car stopped in front of children playing on an unpaved street and Baeming pointed to a house on stilts on our right side.

Hannan's eyes lit up. "Is this the place? I know it!"

We reached the entrance stairs. An old lady sat by the doorway of the porch, wrapped in a batik sarong, her legs gracefully folded to one side. Upon seeing us, she gave us a sweet smile. A tall, middle-aged man emerged and recognised Hannan.

"Where have you been? We haven't seen you for ages!"

It transpired that when Hannan was a boy he had often accompanied his father to the village on Fridays to sell rubber to a Chinese trader. Often they would stay overnight in this house, whose inhabitants were friends of his grandfather, who was the caretaker of the family's orchard. Vague childhood memories of bathing and playing there still remained. Hannan had stopped visiting when he moved to continue his university studies in Pattani and lost contact with the family for years. Not only was he unaware that this household was related to the Raja's lineage, but still less could he have imagined that the 85-year-old lady sitting there, the mother of the man who had received us, was actually the Raja's granddaughter.

She was affectionately called Nor, a Malay term for "mother", a colloquial abbreviation of *Bundor*, an honorific that denoted her aristocratic status. She did not speak Thai, although she could understand it. Hannan introduced me to Nor and her son, explaining that I was interested in Legeh's history. When he added that I was staying at the Rumoh Rajo Legeh, I sensed their puzzlement. Hannan told me later that they could not understand why a Westerner would want to stay in such a derelict place. Nor asked me whether during the night I had heard the footfall of someone plodding about with a heavy limp. According to her, it was a jinn who refused to relieve himself of his duty to the Rajas of Legeh, a dynasty he had loyally served for 500 years. The conversation that afternoon was conducted in Malay, so it wasn't until the meeting was over that Hannan explained to me everything she had said.

From the immemorial times of Langkasuka, the Rajas of Legeh had built several palaces. The house where I stayed, was the last one. The original palace, made of brick and stone, had once been located in present-day Kelantan when the Raja of Legeh was a follower of Hinduism. The wooden palace prior to the one where I was staying had been situated in Tanjong Mas on land that belonged to the family. It was dismantled in the middle of the 19th century, probably as a result of several wars waged between the Malays of Patani and the Siamese. Part of its timber was reused to construct a mosque in Tak Bai and possibly some parts of the new palace in Kampung Takok. The land where the old palace had once stood was now occupied by the army camp we had just passed. It had been set up three years earlier without the family's permission, an act with total impunity that had upset them deeply.

The new palace in Kampung Takok had originally been the residence of the daughter of the Raja of Legeh. It underwent a renovation to the compound by a renowned architect from Terengganu during the second half of the 19th century. Nor's recollections about the house were fragmentary. In the 1930s, she lived there until the age of nine, when she and her mother moved to Tanjong Mas after her parents separated. Nor vaguely remembered the Raja, Tengku Shamsudeen, as an elegant old man clad in white and carrying a walking stick. She corroborated that the Raja had a Malay spouse with whom he had a daughter, his only child, and a Chinese second wife. Although Nor was the granddaughter of the first wife, she was never allowed to enter the Raja's private quarters.

One of her most vivid memories was of a stupendous and sagacious tame elephant, the Raja's favourite. Its black tusks were believed to possess talismanic properties and proof of his unusual intelligence was that he would never allow a menstruating woman to climb on its back. It is said that there was a time when kings were made by elephants. It was a Malay custom that when a ruler died without issue, a sacred elephant was brought to select the successor from among the assembled subjects of the country. Old or young, rich or poor, the one touched by the elephant would be appointed as the future king.

During the splendid cavalcades of old in Legeh, the elephant would be lavishly caparisoned in silk and gold, with an elegant canopy above the howdah bearing his Raja. The elephant was given to Nor's mother in the divorce settlement and went with them to Tanjong Mas. Her family rode on him to the town of Rahman, a 50-kilometre jungle trek that took three days at the time. The extraordinary abilities of the pachyderm reached the ears of a Chinese businessman at the service of the Siamese government, who offered the grand sum of 30,000 baht to buy the elephant. But her mother refused to part with him.

One day the elephant stopped eating. It lay down on the ground with its trunk stretched forward, howling and crying. The mahouts could not find out what was wrong with him. They tried everything to relieve his pain, but to no effect. Unaware that the Raja was seriously ill, they only understood the elephant's behaviour when the sad news from Kampung Takok came a few days later: the Raja had died.

We asked for more details about the Raja and why the house had been neglected but Nor could not remember anything else. Then we asked about Jeh Puteh, the adopted son of the Raja mentioned by Ayoh-ha. Nor confirmed that Jeh Puteh was a

Western man of Dutch origin who had been the Raja's favourite and explained that apart from having been the caretaker, he was irrelevant in the scheme of things. Surprisingly, the legal owner of the house was actually a relative called Kuchi, a woman who also lived in the district. The house had been bequeathed to her with the proviso that it be preserved as a private home or as an Islamic school. Proposals to renovate it had been submitted to the family, including a project sponsored by the U.S. Ambassadors Fund for Cultural Preservation, but they had been rejected because of internal family disagreements concerning the land deed.

That afternoon, Nor's son showed us with pride some of the remnants salvaged from the dismantled palace of Legeh in Tanjong Mas. One of the most remarkable pieces was a large wooden wall panel embellished with moulding, exquisite floral carvings and friezes with Chinese paintings of peonies. However, the objects that impressed me the most were two bronze gongs dating back to the Queens of Patani. Nor told us their names: *Suara Aninyor* (beautiful voice) and *Lalat Hijao* (green fly). Severely corroded, both still radiated a grandeur and solemnity that once might have accompanied the sinuous motions of virgin princesses performing *Asyik* court dance or the dangerous moves of *Silat*[18] fighters. I wondered how long they had been silent.

---

18 *Asyik* (literally "beloved"/"besotted") is a classical royal court dance originated from the Kingdom of Patani. According to Hikayat Patani, the dance was created in 1644 to entertain the grieving Ratu Kuning (Yellow Queen) over the loss of her favorite bird. The dance's name could have been referring to the lost bird.
Silat is an indigenous Malay martial art, whose earliest forms allegedly originated in the Langkasuka Kingdom.

Before leaving, I asked Nor and her son what they knew about Ayoh-ha, expecting to discover some clues as to his identity, his possible ties with the family or if he had been left the house in usufruct. Mother and son glanced at each other in the eye and then simply replied they did not know him. They seemed to hold back, but Hannan did not try to persist in what he sensed might be a thorny matter.

We left the Raja's descendants having learned little about the house and still wondering what had happened to the Raja of Legeh, Tengku Shamsudeen. I began to think that I would never find the answer.

* * *

When I told Ayoh-ha and Faridah of our visit to the family in Tanjong Mas, they made a face of disapproval.

"Impostors," declared Faridah.

They knew well about that family but refused to acknowledge them as the legitimate heirs. Ayoh-ha had always upheld that the only wife of Shamsudeen was a Hainanese woman called Samlee who bore no offspring. If this was true, the family would have descended from one of the members in the household retinue who could have put out a call for spurious ownership claims after the late Raja died childless. The only source that could prove bloodline was the genealogical tree we found in the thesis on the palaces of the seven Malay principalities. The author, Hannan had found out during his visit in Tanjong Mas, was actually Nor's firstborn, a man who held a doctorate in political science and a Member of Parliament for the Democrat party list. We were not equipped to question the claims made by the family, but the political profile of the academic could also raise issues of bias. In the following days, Hannan tried to meet him but he refused, probably wary of the research. The time had come for Ayoh-ha to reveal us his kinship to the rajas.

Before he became the ruler of Legeh, Shamsuddeen once travelled to Bangkok as envoy to dispatch the Bunga Mas, the small tree wrought in gold that Malay rajas paid as tribute to the Siamese kings. One of the members of the delegation was a comely Malay princess from Terengganu called Sied Ku Zaimah, kinswoman to Shamsudeen. Well versed in arts and crafts, Ku Zaimah was loved for her warmth and composure even under the most harrowing of circumstances. The Bunga Mas was not a matter to be taken lightly. In the past, the refusal to dispatch this tribute, considered by Malay rulers a mere token of friendship, but deemed by Siamese kings as a submission to their supremacy, resulted in war between kingdoms. Thus, Shamsudeen commended to Ku Zaimah the care of the golden tree, which she would solemnly yield in person to King Chulalongkorn.

When the steamer departed from the mouth of the Chao Praya River heading back to Legeh, Ku Zaimah was not aboard. She remained in the palace at the request of King Chulalongkorn. Being of the Muslim faith, she was left under the care of the Chularatchamontri, the State Counsellor on Islamic Affairs – a title held by the House of Bunnag, a clan of Persian ancestry in the court of Ayutthaya. According to royal decorum and etiquette, she was given a Siamese name, but allowed to wear her traditional attire and provided with food according to Islamic tenets.

The story of Ku Zaimah was almost identical to that of another Malay princess, once consort to King Mongkut, father of Chulalongkorn. This princess was the half-sister of the Supreme Lord of Riau and Lingga, Sultan Mahmud Muzaffar, who had fled the Dutch and taken refuge in the court of Siam, where he was appointed as the Siamese governor for the Malay states of Kelantan and Terengganu. It was well known that Siamese kings married princesses from tributary dynasties as a means of political leverage. Such pursuit of spousal bonds entailed recompense to the parties involved, so it was not surprising that Shamsudeen was eventually appointed as the new Raja of Legeh, soon after Ku Zaimah entered the court of Siam.

The young princess lived in the Vimanmek Palace hoping to return to her home one day, a dream that faded as the years went by. Her family always awaited her homecoming. Perhaps trying to make her happy, the king eventually enabled her to live in a lake house within the royal compound, where the cooler air and beautiful lotus floating around the building would surely inspire the pursuit of her artistic callings. Ku Zaimah ended her days within those walls and was buried in the cemetery adjacent to Ton Son mosque, the oldest in Bangkok, built in the Ayutthaya era. Only death freed her from imposed seclusion. Who would have said that her grand-nephew would today be in custody of what was left of her homeland?

The story, given the confidentiality of sensitive kingly matters, would be extremely difficult to corroborate. My friend consulted with a professor in Bangkok who was doing research on the consorts of King Chulalongkorn, and confirmed the existence of the only one of Muslim faith called Chao Chom Lamai. Were both women the same person? We probably will never know.

Whatever the truth was, I had never seen the heirs visiting the house, nor had they evinced any interest in its preservation, unlike Ayoh-ha who had consecrated himself and his own resources to conserve it and its spirit.

By now, my ties with Ayoh-ha and Faridah had grown so strong that I expressed my emotions to them without thinking. Seized by a sudden rapture, I would jump up, and describe with passion my impressions of the house and how my heart had found rest wrapped by its light and shadows, while they sat on the floor, listening to my words, captivated, smiling with a tender gaze. During those moments of elation, I would become childlike with Ayoh-ha, hugging him and kissing him on the cheek, as if he were my father.

"I know you love this house," Faridah told me with a gratifying smile.

I think she had known since the beginning, since my very first visit alone that afternoon a year ago, that I was there not because of them. I was not there because of my deep affection for the family and for Ayoh-ha, or because of my fondness for the town and its people or even my brotherhood with Hannan; I was there for the sake of the house. It was only now I could accept this was the sole reason: my strange bond to this place.

Faridah had told me several times how blessed I was because not everyone could live in the Rumoh Rajo. My nights were restful while others would have suffered from unnatural illnesses or visions of death. Whoever was able to sleep at the house seemed somehow related to the Rajas. Time could never sever those atavistic ties that, no matter how distant they were, would endow a related person the right to live in the erstwhile palace without disturbances. Then she mentioned my heritage. Months ago, I had told her of my mother's homeland, Andalusia, once a prosperous land ruled for hundreds of years by the Moors, Al-Andalus. Ayoh-ha nodded at the name, and talked of his own roots. His forefathers had travelled from Morocco through Arabia and India to the Moluccas, where his grandmother was born, during the Dutch East Indies era, in the bosom of the Sultanate of Surakarta. She married an aristocrat from Patani and settled there. Ayoh-ha asserted that we might well share Moorish ancestry. Despite my doubts, I placated him with a smile.

"Now you know why you can stay here," Faridah said.

As the three of us sat chatting about the past, the conversation swerved into the future, when they began to talk about it as if I were going to stay for good. They saw me as the instrument, the driving force behind the palace's ultimate restoration. I listened to their portrayal of a future where we lived together in the house as a happy family, unconcerned with anything or anyone outside. Speaking in unison with an excitement that tantalised me, their words expressed a conviction that they could persuade me to leave my world and embrace theirs forever. I was unable to reply but just kept staring at them, listening with a mixture of joy and unease. Despite my qualms, I became possessed by their bizarre idea of a plausible life together and my imagination flew far into the future: in the blink of my mind's eye, I saw myself spending my remaining years in the solitude of this derelict palace.

* * *

By January's end, the storms became less frequent and more forgiving. The sun's first attempts to dry the wood began in-between the gentler showers. Sprawled on the bamboo bench in the rear hall, I would slip into reverie, watching how rain poured hard all at once only to weaken after a short while, transformed into a diaphanous silky screen that swayed in the air.

On Sunday, a vast swath of ink washed lazily over the canvas of the sky, but, knowing it would not rain, I spent a calm afternoon in Ao Manao, returning earlier than usual because Hannan expected me for dinner with his family.

I was riding to his house and about to reach the clock-tower junction when two blasts resonated behind me, one after another.

I stopped dead in my tracks, turned back and saw a glow opposite the morning market, several metres from me. I sprinted towards the spot and dropped my bicycle nearby. Children were crying and adults were fleeing in all directions. A building was in flames. A plume of smoke spouted from the entrance above shattered glass and debris. It was the supermarket where I often shopped. I dashed closer to take pictures. The fire raged. Flames fluttered through windows, curling and twisting higher, crackling, baking the pavement, inflaming the air, scorching my skin. In minutes, the blaze had leapt up the four-storey structure. Sirens and flashing lights joined the pandemonium as an ambulance rushed to the scene, hesitated for a second and then left swiftly. A pick-up sped in its wake, braking hard. Five men leaped out, manned a hose and aimed at the blazing inferno. Water leaked from the hose clamp, spilling everywhere. Their efforts looked futile. A man ran back and forth screaming, gesticulating frantically.

Finally, a fire truck arrived. Soldiers, militia and police appeared everywhere, taking up positions, holding back bystanders and, within minutes, sealing off that section of the street while others around me, perhaps reporters, took photos and video. A young woman stood beside me with a camcorder in her shaking hands, filming and shedding tears.

"We've never seen anything like this in the town centre," she said in a quivering voice.

"There are still people inside the store!" someone else shouted.

I knew the employees well from our long chats in the shop and feared they were still inside. Burned to death. The thought of it made me sick. I stood transfixed, taking in the horrific, unreal scene. At some point, I remembered my dinner with Hannan and Pu. They were expecting me and were surely worried. I tried to call them to say that I was safe, but the signal had been cut off, the usual military procedure in a bombing situation. I grabbed my bicycle and rode fast to their house, only 400 metres from the blaze. The entire family was standing on the street in front of their home like many others, relieved to see me after trying to call me many times. They told me that there had been a concerted three-pronged attack on the town.

First, gunmen had killed some militiamen on a bridge checkpoint in Yakang, just three kilometres away from Hannan's parents' house. Then came the detonations, whose aftermath I had witnessed, which destroyed the Jintai store, while a second bomb had exploded at the Sui Hua store a few blocks away. There were also rumours of another bomb being diffused further down the road next to an ice cream shop. Hannan explained all this with nervous excitement rather than fear. The children did not look scared either, although they knew what was going on. Hannan asked me to download the pictures I had taken to post on his Facebook page. The internet connection was blocked right after he had done it.

The mayhem left us all exhausted and hungry and we decided to have dinner somewhere in town as far away from the area as we could. Hannan drove, but as we reached the clock-tower roundabout, an army blockade forced us to take the only road open, heading south towards Yakang bridge where the first of the attacks had taken place. Just before reaching the bridge checkpoint, Hannan made a U-turn to avoid the hassle of an inspection, but despite taking a detour, he could not dodge another checkpoint that had been set up on the fringes of the town.

We were stopped. Soldiers shone flashlights on our faces from both sides of the car. I wondered how they would react to seeing a Westerner but they did not seem to pay much attention to me. The soldiers asked for identification from Hannan and performed a cursory check. There was a moment of tension because he could not produce his I.D. card but after he showed his teacher's card, everything was fine. We were waved through.

Thereafter, a sweeping bypass took us to the dark outskirts of town and our car, the only one on the road, plunged into an eerie, unbroken expanse of emptiness. We came to a large junction lit by a few lampposts. I asked Hannan to stop for a minute so I could get out of the car for some fresh air. The rough surface of the tarmac flared with the brake lights. It was deadly silent. A traffic light timer blinked its countdown in red numbers...54, 53, 52, 51. In the distance, under a lucent dome in the middle of the crossing, appeared the scraggy shadow of a lone goat like a harbinger of doom.

Finally, we found a place to eat. The five of us, the only customers in the restaurant, did not talk much, buried in our plates. By the time I headed back to the house on my bicycle, it was already past midnight, on a moonless night, the streets a thoroughfare of desolation and the air cooler than usual, as if autumn had exiled from Europe to settle over Narathiwat.

I did not encounter a soul on my way back to Kampung Takok, only street dogs and alley cats roaming around. Most of them scurried away as I passed, except one jet-black cat that stood like an Egyptian statuette on the footpath with such poise and presence that I could not help but stop in front of him. The cat turned his head left and right as if watching something passing along the road, although there was nothing there, or at least, nothing I could see. Even when I moved nearer, my stare piercing his golden eyes, the cat ignored me and kept surveying the road. Only after coming really close did he step back. I carried on homeward, gazing back at him several times while riding down the road, and each time I did, he was still there, sitting immobile, stoic, his eyes on me.

A mirage of the events loitered in the drowsy world of the Rumoh Rajo. I found Ayoh-ha standing in the middle of the hall with a scowl on his face as though as he had been waiting for me, but he did not spare a word. Instead, he just motioned his head towards Faridah's room. I knew too well that asking him what he meant would have been pointless, so I nodded. Peering in, I found her asleep. Maybe she had been worried about me. I was too tired to work out what was going on. Taking refuge in my room, I flopped down on my bed, exhausted.

The next morning I took an early cycle ride to get a feel of the town in the bombings' aftermath. The park, normally crowded by six o'clock, was nearly empty. I asked the militiaman on duty at the gates why that was, despite already knowing the answer.

"It rained," he replied, assuming I was a newcomer.

Traffic in town was scarce and many shops were closed. I decided to go for breakfast at my favourite Chinese teahouse whose owner I had met almost a year earlier with Abdul Ghani, the man who had first taken me to the house. I parked in front of the orange car bomb barrier, a sight that had been ordinary, almost invisible, until today. The owner sat in the back, brooding in the shadows, looking at an empty cup of tea on his table.

I recalled months ago, listening untroubled to his warnings about how dangerous it was for me to ride around alone on a bicycle – killing a foreigner would make headlines.

Calling me over, he gestured for me to sit with him, seeming both reluctant and eager to talk. After a minute, his silence broke.

"See? They targeted shops owned by Thai-Chinese!" I wanted to say something but I knew my words would not help. He fell silent before adding, "How about the market? Bombs only explode on the Buddhist side! Do you know why? They want us to leave!" He was seething with rage and after discharging his anger refused to say any more. I left him alone and had my breakfast.

That morning military blockades still restricted access to the wrecked stores, but I found a way to reach the main road via a small back street behind the market. The Jintai grocery store I had seen burning the night before was now a charred heap, an acrid smell hanging thick in the hot air. Parked in front was a fire truck and ambulances while inside the building a bomb disposal team, uniformed policemen and plain-clothes investigators sifted through the rubble for evidence.

Among the crowd of bystanders I bumped into some people I knew, such as Jong, the young owner of the Kodak shop where I printed my photographs. While he was taking pictures, I could read on his face how disturbed he was. "You know, my staff told me that last Friday a guy came into the shop asking if we had a CCTV system," he told me.

"Please be careful," was all I could say to him.

One of the girls who had worked in the store was watching. Luckily, yesterday was her day off. As she stood wondering whether any of her workmates had died, a man walked past and turning to her, he giggled, saying, "Where will you work now?" She did not reply.

A husband, his pregnant wife and their three-year old son had died in the fire. They were Muslim neighbours in Kampung Takok who lived near the House of the Raja. I stood watching medics remove their bodies in black plastic bags and load them into the ambulances. I imagined myself in one of those bags. It was not a far fetched thought, as I had been in the shop to buy snacks for the children only the day before the bombing and at the same time. I also went to see what was left of the Sui Hua supermarket, a few blocks down the street. There was a crane truck, soldiers and another bomb squad walking among debris. A silent crowd watched. The fire had also gutted this building, much larger than the other one. I overheard from onlookers that the bombs could have been incendiary devices and that the owner of this store had died while trying to save some of his merchandise. A 24-year-old Muslim teacher from Yingo also had died, hit by the blast when passing by on motorbike. Hannan had known her. The next day, I went with him to the cemetery opposite his house to attend her burial ceremony.

A group of men had gathered at the site while women watched on the outside through an iron gate.

"Women are not allowed in to avoid their making a scene, it's our custom," Hannan explained to me.

I did not see any tears. Clothed all in white, the *babo* (headmaster) of her school sat cross-legged in front of a burial mound praying in the customary position, the palms of his hands upwards facing his chin. After praying he gently poured water onto the grave. When the funeral attendees dispersed, I saw that Azman was among them. I had not seen him since that evening tea with his friend Abdul, a few months ago. It seemed decades.

"How are you?" he asked me, shaking my hand while brandishing his abounding smile, despite all. The victim was a far relative of his. We gave him our condolences.

We wended our way out, negotiating a clutter of gravestones in the shape of fingertip bones that crawled up through weeds trying to reach for us. My friend pointed at the oldest ones. We paused in front of a mark cut in wood with inscriptions in Jawi that could be more than two hundred years old. While staring at this grave, whittled over years of floods and droughts, the words of a shopkeeper in Yala who I met, having recently arrived in the Deep South, came to my mind.

"The first year, when violence erupted, was the toughest one, but now, 10 years later, when someone dies from a gunshot or the explosion of a bomb, it's thought of as one more accident". Violent death had become trivial in the Deep South.

The next day, more than 30 bombs rattled through the neighbouring city of Yala, killing three and injuring dozens, while later that week, newspapers reported that insurgents had carried out the attacks in Narathiwat, although no one had publicly claimed responsibility. All kind of rumours circulated among locals who seemed disinclined to believe the official version. Facing an escalation in the violence, the military stepped up security measures, increasing its presence and setting up new checkpoints across town-centre streets, including at the clock-tower crossing. This only added to the atmosphere of tension.

During the days following the incident, the pervasive gloom and grief hanging over the town overwhelmed me. It felt like a reminder of constantly impending danger. What a fool I had been! Narathiwat was not the sleepy town I had believed it to be. It was all an illusion. The veneer of innocence was breached. Until then, although I had been aware of the conflict, I had expunged it from my consciousness. Before the bombings, danger was a remote possibility, but now the hitherto vague and distant conflict was tangible and immediate. It was only a matter of time until something else happened. It could be tomorrow, any day of next week or next month and there was absolutely nothing I could do about it. This made me reflect on how unwary I had been, going around carefree, overlooking basic safety measures.

From then on I resolved to be more careful: avoiding morning markets at early times when they were most crowded; not visiting grocery stores and the 7-Elevens after six in the evening, which meant buying my supplies before nighttime; staying away from security forces and government posts in the early morning or late evening. It took a while until the initial fear waned, when I began to see things from a different perspective: witnessing violence with my own eyes was the best way to understand what the locals had been enduring for years as part of their daily lives..

* * *

A week after the incident, I was chilling out in the foyer when I heard someone addressing Faridah, who sat by the doorway.

"Can we talk?"

I went to see who was there, only to find that four heavily armed soldiers wearing bulletproof vests had come up on the verandah, while two more remained positioned at the foot of the staircase. One of the soldiers, who could speak Malay, had been part of the contingent that months ago had raided the house. They showed no surprise at seeing me, as if they already knew a foreigner was staying there. Indeed, a few weeks earlier, Faridah had told me that during my absence, a party of police officers had shown up inquiring about me.

A captain introduced himself as an army doctor, explaining that they were there to carry out a routine check on every household in the vicinity. The officer said that he was curious about the building and casually asked to have a look inside. In a deliberate display of respect, they removed their boots and took off their helmets before entering, but carried their assault rifles with them. Ayoh-ha came out of his room and received them in such an obsequious way that it looked almost comical to me. During the time they spent there, it was all kind smiles, polite words and good manners, but I knew that this was all part of a skillfully staged play. Before leaving, the captain even gave away his flashlight to Ayoh-ha as a memento. I was relieved when they were gone.

That same week, a navy lieutenant, accompanied by two armed soldiers, suddenly turned up at Hannan's house. From the badges on his uniform, he could tell it was an information operation officer and that this was not exactly a courtesy visit. They exchanged polite greetings whilst they both stood staring at each other, mute with stupefaction. The officer happened to be a local Malay who had been Hannan's junior in high school and this was their first encounter since their graduation. With a dazed expression still on his face upon the odd reunion, the lieutenant began patting his pockets, mumbled something about an urgent phone call and hastily left.

They would meet again a few weeks later in a 7-Eleven store, apparently by chance. This time, Hannan had no qualms to ask him straight away the motive of his visit and how he came to join the military. His friend replied with an unsound, "Oh, I was just passing by and wanted to say hello." He went on to explain that he had qualified with honours in journalism and worked for a newspaper in Bangkok for a year until a good friend of him who was doing well in the navy encouraged him to enlist. Then, his face turned serious.

"You know you are being followed, don't you? There will be trouble ahead if you get involved in shady deals."

His blunt words, surely the actual reason for the hasty visit, did not surprise Hannan. His keen research on local histories had obviously drawn the attention of the military and he was aware that some of the people he interviewed might have links with separatist organisations or even belong to one. In the view of the men in green that amounted to consorting with the enemy. Hannan replied that he was not doing anything wrong, albeit he knew too well things didn't work that way in the Deep South. Incriminating someone upon false charges was a common ploy used by the military. Before leaving, his former junior warned him once again.

"It doesn't matter you are clean or not, you know they can mess with you if they want to, so just take care of yourself."

* * *

We were running out of rice, so Faridah sent me to the Chinese grocery store by the roadside where we used to buy some of our supplies. I was about to leave when a man came up to me. He lived just across the street but, oddly, I had never seen him until then. Eager to practice his English, he wanted to know about the only foreigner in the area and asked me if I was afraid to come there. When I told him I was staying at the Rumoh Rajo Legeh, he looked impressed and replied that I ought to meet his father, who, he asserted, knew a great deal about local history. I nodded to please him, hoping he would leave me alone. He might have sensed my lack of interest because he became so insistent that I agreed to arrange a meeting. One evening that week, Hannan and I reluctantly went to hear what his father had to tell us.

The old gentleman, whose name was Tok Wae, actually lived just a few doors away from Hannan, although, much to his surprise, they had never happened to meet each other. A man dressed in traditional Malay attire welcomed us into a small, modest timber house. He wore a white *kopiah*, a sienna check sarong perfectly tied to his slender body and a vintage long-sleeved collarless shirt, worn in the old days only by aristocrats – inherited from his grandfather, we would learn later. I discerned a strangely familiar candour in his hazel eyes, serene and profound. He motioned us inside, carrying himself with placid graciousness.

"Welcome to my humble home, come in please" he said in fluent English with an American accent that felt out of place in such surroundings. The small sitting room had posters of Mecca on the wall and old books on a corner shelf. Hannan cast his eye over the latter, finding amongst them an English paperback edition of Islamic art in Spain by a defunct Japanese publisher I happened to know.

"Your country!" He said pointing to it excitedly.

Tok Wae offered us a seat on a couch and when he mentioned he was 72, I remarked that he looked very good for his age.

"I know how to take good care of myself," he said. "I get a lot of exercise riding my bicycle and, besides tea, I drink only purified water, not less than two litres a day. By the way, would you like a glass of water?"

This was quite unusual, as hosts always offered tea in other Muslim homes. I thought that perhaps he considered it unnecessary to behave in the customary fashion with a foreigner. It was an odd little detail, but one that set the tone of what was to be a bizarre meeting.

I could not help but ask him about his excellent English.

"Oh, I learned it many years ago, in my student days. That was during the Vietnam War. I used to work as a waiter at a restaurant in Bangkok frequented by American soldiers where I was also in charge of the flicks. We screened movies day and night. I loved them! With this job, I could also pay for my studies."

"You must have very interesting stories to tell" I said, hoping to hear more about his life during those times of upheaval.

"You bet. There was much happening back in the Sixties. The U.S. government poured millions into Thailand to build highways, dams, airports, railways, hospitals, you name it. Anyway, the Thai aid program skyrocketed and there was a great deal of work to do. A military advisor, who was a regular at the restaurant and very fond of me, pulled some strings for me to join a team working with Chevron on an oil and gas exploration project in the Gulf of Thailand. Eventually, speaking fluent English, Arabic and Malay took me to be the first Thai to join Aramco in Saudi Arabia, where I served as the CEO's personal assistant. As you can imagine, from there my career took off. Those were hardworking and very stressful years. My subordinates grew jealous of me and I got tired of watching my back. I missed Narathiwat, so I came home and married."

He continued casually chatting about himself for a while until he finally sat in front of us and, thrusting a stare at me like a spear, abruptly asked, "So why are you interested in that house?"

I told him as best I could about my journeys through the Deep South, how I had come across the building, the feelings it had awoken in me, my obsessive attachment and also how I had met Hannan and his role in the whole story. He listened attentively, nodding, his hazel eyes penetrating mine. It dawned on me that he already knew everything I was saying and that strange feeling grew stronger as I approached the end of my account.

When I finished my story, he averted his gaze, lowered his head and proclaimed, "The spirit of the owner of the house is with us now."

Hannan turned to me with wide-open eyes. Before we could reply, Tok Wae placed his hands on his chest and began to recite words in Malay that I could not understand, but which the next day Hannan translated for me:

> *"Minta izinlah Tokku*
> *Aku kan cerita kepada ia*
> *Apa yang aku tahu*
> *Seorang lagi bukan yang lain*
> *Anak cucu juga"*

> *"I ask permission from you, grandfather,*
> *to tell them what I know*
> *including this man,*
> *who's your child, too"*

After his recitation, he lapsed into silence for a few seconds before addressing us. He explained that his grandfather had been a prominent Mufti, a Sunni Islamic scholar and legal adviser to the Raja, and that he had kept many of his personal documents and books.

"You will know about my ancestors at the proper time, but meanwhile I can only tell you about the Raja, Tengku Shamsudeen. I want to show you something," Tok Wae said.

He rose, went to another room, and returned with a manuscript and a book he handed to Hannan. The book in Thai and Jawi was a chronological compilation of missives handwritten by King Chulalongkorn. Between the endpapers was a sepia-toned photograph of his grandfather in a black tunic and turban standing in a field beside a man clad in white, leaning on his walking stick – Tengku Shamsudeen. The manuscript was a compendium from Siamese sources about the policies implemented in the South at the turn of the last century. Hannan read the summary, its contents the answer to the mystery that had been devouring me...

In 1902, the Kingdom of Siam annexed the Seven Malay Principalities in the South to unify the country and to safeguard its sovereignty against the encroachments of the French and British colonial powers. King Chulalongkorn conferred full power on a governor-general from the House of Bunnag to depose the seven Rajas, ending their sole authority over the principalities. Shamsudeen, along with other Malay rulers, opposed the reform. He wrote a letter to Sir Swettenham, Governor of the Straits Settlements requesting his intercession. But, albeit critical of Bangkok's policies over the Malay states, the British had their hands tied over these matters since the previously signed Bowring Treaty promised non-interference in Siam's affairs. Fearing an uprising, the Siamese governor-general deployed the Royal Navy gunships at Bukit Tanjong, present-day Ao Manao. A steam warship detachment headed up the Bang Nara River and anchored in front of the Palace of Legeh. Newspapers across the region reported the incident. *The Straits Times* in Singapore published it under the heading, "Rajas kidnapped in Siam":

On March 18 of 1902, H.H., the Raja of Legeh, with a suite of about eight men, was abducted by Phraya Sukhumnaiwinit, the Siamese Commissioner of Singgora and brought there in a Siamese gunboat.

The Siamese commissioner disembarked accompanied by armed soldiers and first read a letter from the King of Siam in which he promised to give the Raja 20,000 ticals (whilom Thai baht) annually. He then produced a document with the obnoxious clause as to deposition, and new rules for the government of the country. His Highness asked for time to consider and consult his council, but this was refused. He was then given five minutes and told if he did not sign, he would be deposed then and there. Still refusing, Phraya Sukhum then said he should appoint Tengku Pitak (a pro-Siamese very fond of gambling) as Raja. He said the arrangement was only temporary, once more asked the Raja to sign, and as he still refused, called up soldiers, and under the drawn swords of these men, the Raja was conducted straight on board the gunboat, being allowed no time either to see his family or get any clothes.

People congregated at the pier in a desperate attempt to prevent soldiers from taking away their Raja. Fearing bloodshed, Shamsudeen made a plea of non-resistance, asking them to go home. People stayed at the pier to see the gunboat carrying their Raja steam away, until it faded out of sight.

The whole episode entered into history in Siamese annals as "The Treason of Rajas of Seven Malay States".

Close family and friends spent weeks in Singgora, imploring for his release in vain. Shamsudeen was held for a year without a shadow of a trial. British journalists from Singapore visited Legeh, enquiring about the Raja. The Siamese authority would answer that he was away, devoted to the study of Thai language. Tengku Abdul Kadir, Raja of Patani state, shared the same fate, abducted and brought to Pitsanulok, where he was imprisoned for more than two years before going into exile to Kelantan.

During the captivity of the rajas, the Malay Principalities were disbanded, their currencies, administrative units and armies abolished to be integrated into Siam as a monthon[19], Legeh being the last state to fall and Shamsudeen, the last of the Rajas.

No communication was permitted between the Raja and his subjects. Only a few telegrams would be able to reach His Highness and answers were received ostensibly from him. The Siamese consistently refused to allow any messengers to see him personally, but from an unofficial report, His Highness seemed

---

19 The *monthon* was a bureaucratic administrative system introduced in 1897 by the first Siamese Minister of Interior, Prince Damrong Rajanubhab, marking the transition from the old tributary system to the administrative division of Siam that formed the basis of modern Thailand.

to be in good health, and to be taking care not to expose his life to any danger. The same went for the rest of the Rajas who had refused to abide. Two emissaries to the Raja of Patani, imprisoned in Pitsanulok, left on a steamer called the "Monliut" that was going directly to Bangkok. The boat, however, stopped at Singgora and they were transferred to the "ChamToen" which, unfortunately, sank and the men, including the Raja Muda (crown prince) of Rahman drowned.

That same year Buddhist-Siamese troops were sent to counterbalance the Malay-Muslim majority and an intelligence division was created to keep abreast of developments in the South. In 1905, the Bunga Mas, the golden tree tribute that the Malay Rajas had been dispatching every three years to the Siamese king was discontinued by royal edict, and replaced by an inflated poll tax that was to be collected annually from every Malay.

One of the missives Hannan translated was an offer by King Chulalongkorn to release the Raja on condition that he swear allegiance to Siam and renounce any future involvement in politics. After the treaty, the Raja returned as a commoner to his home and a country that was no more. Of all the deposed Rajas, only Shamsudeen stayed in his residence, for he wanted to spend his last days on his land among his people.

Legeh had once been a rich country. With a tonne of annual gold exports to Bangkok and Singapore, it had had the highest-valued currency among the Seven Principalities and levied its own taxes. Now, entirely in Siamese hands, its inhabitants were subjected to abuses of power by Bangkok officials. They were squeezed under a multifarious taxation system and many were dispossessed of their farms and businesses, their revenue diverted to Siamese headquarters leaving nothing for the benefit of the Malays. The *Khaluang Yai* (High Commissioner) imposed the *Kra,* a forced labour system, abolished years earlier by King Chulalongkorn. Men, including village headmen, were dragged from their paddies, fishing boats and even from the mosques, to build roads and houses for the Siamese. Those who refused to work were jailed and replaced by their wives. No wages were paid. Many flew to Kelantan.

Although the region was now under administrative rule from Bangkok, the Raja's former subjects still recognised only his authority and kept visiting the palace seeking his guidance. But he was no longer in the position to meddle in what were now affairs of the Siamese state. Deeply frustrated, Shamsudeen travelled by train to Bangkok several times to appeal for an audience with the king, his despair growing with each rejection. As the years went by, Shamsudeen depleted his wealth to help his people as much as he could. Overcome by his failure, the Raja, now a broken man, took solace in opium – in those days traded legally. Shamsudeen's health slowly declined and when he died in his quarters, some say of sorrow, a long ancestry of rulers that once enjoyed the splendour of the fabled Langkasuka became a shade with him.

Even though he had been stripped of his position, Shamsudeen was mourned according to his status. Following the Malay-Muslim tradition, his body was washed using leaves, then anointed and swathed in cloth and placed in a bamboo coffin filled with river sand. The coffin lay in state in the attic of his residence for seven days so other former Rajas could come to pay their respect. Every night, cannons in Kampung Takok and Tanjong Mas fired five farewell salvoes. Thousands of mourners joined the cortège that stretched for miles. More than 100 pallbearers carried the Raja's coffin, conveyed on the Royal Chariot and on which nine eminent Imams rode. One of those Imams was Hannan's grandfather.

We knew the rest of the story: the heirs sold off plots of land, dependencies were torn down and the old palace, bereft of the Raja's presence, began to deteriorate. Servants gradually left, abandoning the building to plunder and decay until only shadows inhabited it. The construction of a new road diverted the growth of Narathiwat town away from the forsaken palace and Shamsudeen's name fell into oblivion.

Hannan's eyes brimmed with tears when he finished reading.

Tok Wae broke the silence first. "Shortly before this region was taken over, Shamsudeen requested to meet my father in the grounds of one of his coconut plantations. Using the tip of his walking stick, he marked in the dirt where the first pillar of a new mosque was to be built as a memorial and said to my father, 'You must bury me here in this land, not anywhere else.' I am sure he could already sense that his life was coming to its end. Two weeks later he fell gravely ill and passed away in the house, where his spirit would linger. That mosque was his *Wassiyah* (last will)."

A mausoleum was erected over the Raja's tomb in the immediate vicinity to where the mosque would sit, the very same old mosque topped with a green dome that now stood across from the clock-tower. Every night when I had made my way from Hannan's home back to the House of the Raja, I had passed his grave without knowing it.

"When I go to the mosque and pass by the Raja's tomb, I always say, 'Assalamualaikum Tengku.' Before leaving on a trip, I ask for his blessing and then I know everything will be fine. Sometimes, when the smell of sandalwood incense comes to me, I know it's my Raja. Whenever I pray, the old Rajas are with me."

His gaze now fell on me and he added, "There is a reason behind what you said about your trip and this house."

"What do you mean?" I asked, at a loss.

"You and Hannan have not met by chance. You both have been called."

"Called by who? For what?"

"The house. The house has called upon you to revive its memories and bring back its lost glory."

His words caught me off guard, impressing me deeply. It sounded rather fantastical, but I did not feel I should argue. In fact, I felt an irrepressible wish to give credence to his words.

"Why should I have been chosen instead of a local? Why should a foreigner be entrusted with the Raja's legacy?" I asked, surprised with my own questions and my willingness to believe the answers.

"Precisely because you are a foreigner. The local people had forgotten about the palace. For them it's just an old derelict house. Even I have forgotten and have not been there for more than 40 years. Only an outsider could arouse new interest, someone with an artistic vision, a sensibility for the unseen and with the ability to transmit what he can see to others. You have opened the door of this house to Hannan, and Hannan will become the bridge through which this knowledge will be transferred to others."

Tok Wae reached for a book on the corner shelf and handed it to me. It was the same book Hannan had seen earlier, an old English edition titled, "The Alhambra", the magnificent Islamic palace built by the Moors in Granada, Spain.

"I know that you have Muslim blood from your mother's side. I am sure your ancestors were from Morocco or Algeria. At some point, your Islamic roots were cut but they have brought you here."

With this mysterious revelation our visit came to a close. Hannan and I were speechless after what we had heard. The old man accompanied us to the door saying, "God did not give us eyes to see the spirits that dwell among us. How could we live in this world if we were able to see them? We would go insane. But there is no doubt that there are other worlds within this one, and there are good and bad spirits, such as angels and Satan."

"How do you feel about the spirit that is with us now?" I asked him.

"I feel good ... warm."

"That means that the Raja has accepted me?"

"I think so, though at the same time he finds you strange."

Before we left, he politely asked me to return again, but at the door his face turned serious and he warned me, "Please keep what I have told you to yourself."

It was after this encounter, riding away on my bicycle through the dark streets of the town, the silence broken only by the sound of my tyres through puddles, that my perception of myself began to acquire an awkward dimension. I felt my identity diluting, blending with the cool air. It was a new and unexpected feeling of a kind I had never experienced, but I knew it had been stirred by the old man's words: the incredible idea that I had been summoned by the spirits of the house to fulfil their desire to revive its memory, to restore its lost consciousness. It implied that every step taken on my journey had been guided.

I recalled all my chance encounters with those who were somehow related to the house and how everything seemed to be falling into place. From the beginning of my travels in the Deep South, I had been recording my experiences in a journal, but now it occurred to me that I was no longer the author of my own story. If that were true and I was not the narrator, but a mere character gliding through the pages and hence my experiences written beforehand, then my choices had already been made and the events to come had already taken place. Past and future overlapped, merging into an absolute present. That night, I felt liberated from the burden of the past and the anxiety of the future.

* * *

On arriving at the house, I found the entrance door wide open. It struck me as unusual as it normally remained closed during nighttime. Wondering if someone had come to visit, I looked around but there were no unfamiliar shoes by the entrance. I closed the door behind me and walked across shadows. One of the lamps in Faridah's room was lit as usual. She never turned it off. I peered inside and saw her asleep, cocooned in the netting, coiled in her bedspread. Next to her was Ayoh-ha, lying supine with stretched limbs, his arms alongside his dark body without the slightest motion of breathing. Indeed, he was so still, that for a moment he appeared devoid of life. My gaze remained on him, exploring the texture of his face, waxy and coarse like that of an embalmed corpse. Suddenly his torso started to expand and contract, as if the waves sent by my gaze had resurrected him.

I decided to go to my room, but as I was about to lie down, I heard heavy footsteps in the hall. It might be Ayoh-ha, who liked feeding his goldfish in the courtyard pond at the most awkward times, I thought. But, when I opened the door to look outside, I saw no one, and so went back into my room, lay down and fell asleep as soon as I closed my eyes.

Sometime later that night I awoke for no apparent reason. It had happened before but this time was different. I could not move. My body was numb and paralysed, as though it were not mine. Strangely, I could feel my left hand. Something or someone held it. Its grip tightened every now and then as if whatever, or whoever, it was, wanted to communicate through contact. I panicked and tried lifting my arms but they would not respond. Gathering all my strength, I attempted to raise myself up but no matter how hard I tried, my muscles refused to budge even a millimetre, as if under a massive weight that kept me glued to the bed. Then, I realised that the head was the only part of my body that responded to me. It did not make sense. My breath ragged. I felt the urge to look to my left, and when I did, I saw a white formless shape emerge out of the darkness. I could describe it as a cloud of gas but it had a strange consistency, flowing at will in space. I turned back quickly, stunned. My heart pounded hard and fast as if desperately trying to awaken my still inert body. This was not a dream. A soft breath whispered in my ear. I had to rid myself of whatever had seized me. Terrified, I opened my mouth to scream, but no matter how hard I tried to strain my throat, only silence filled the room. Suddenly, I felt the presence leaving. A crescendo followed, surging out of my lungs and through my gaping mouth from a moan to a howl of agony.

I have no idea how long I continued to scream or if anyone heard me, but no one came to my room. My body had come back to life, but I dared not get up. The heavy beats of my heart still thumped in my stomach and my temples for a long while. Sleep came only after a few hours out of sheer exhaustion.

The next morning, Faridah announced that something urgent had come up and that she and Ayoh-ha were going north to Nakhon Si Thammarat to see some relatives for a few days. She asked me if I could look after the house. The short notice surprised me. Such a sudden trip was most unusual, as they seldom left the place and if they did, never went very far. It meant I would be sleeping in the house alone. I immediately thought of my night terror, which I preferred to remember as the worst nightmare of my life. I, nevertheless, agreed to stay.

That same day, I spent the afternoon outside with Hannan. My friend had been admitted to a master's degree program at Prince of Songkla University in Pattani and wanted to celebrate the good news with a family dinner. I was very happy for him. When I asked him why he decided to continue his studies, he told me that his work at the school was more interesting now that he could share in class what he had learned about local histories and that he owed it all to the rediscovery of the house. But what had heartened him to attain higher grounds was the last obnoxious example of sophistry.

The principal at his school had grown suspicious of his history teachings, which in his view, diverged dangerously from that of the authorised version. On one occasion, he crouched behind the classroom door to eavesdrop on Hannan while he was enlightening his students with how the Kingdom of Siam annexed Patani. Outraged, the director lodged a complaint against him to the provincial governor's office. Summoned a few days later by the board, Hannan was admonished against the pitfall of teachings that, in the words of the education secretariat's staff, "created confusion among students", on the grounds that glossing over the past was the only way to move forward. Hannan was of a different opinion. To him, education meant to acknowledge the past to be able to understand the present and confront the future.

Months later, things would even out, when the school director attended an important seminar on history and culture chaired by an eminent professor from Silpakorn Univeristy in Bangkok and was shocked to see that his underling was a guest speaker.

* * *

I return late after waiting for the rain to let up. My arrival is met with a chorus of frogs swirling across the swampy meadows around the house. Usually, the lamps remain lit all night by the entrance as well as in Faridah's room, but this evening there is no light except for the full moon glowing behind a thin veil of clouds that casts its pale haze over the gables. Under that dim glow, the house gives off its greatest aura of solitude and I fancy I am the first visitor in many years. I climb the staircase, remove my shoes and put them aside carefully. Pushing the door inward, I feel the embrace of shadows drawing me in.

When I was a child, darkness frightened me. It still does. Not the darkness of night, deep in a deserted alley or in the heart of a forest, but the deep shadows that dwelt in our home, in our corridor, behind doors, inside my bedroom. In the familiar space of our flat in Barcelona, the dark was an invisible tenant under whose watch we lived. I could never have imagined that in a strange house thousands of kilometres away from home, I would encounter that same darkness, this time without fear. Tonight, I want to surrender myself to the arms of this darkness, to feel the recesses of the house without seeing them.

I creep through the shadows of the foyer to reach the door leading into the central hall and turn the knob slowly. Reaching the back, I decide not to climb upstairs yet and head instead to the courtyard to perform a ritual ablution before entering the inner sanctum of the house.

Naked trees accompany me, their branches cupped in supplication, reaching up to the moonlit pall above. The touch of cool water from the well on my skin makes me shiver. After bathing, I put on a dry sarong and pause to look up the staircase lit by the meagre light behind me, its last steps disappearing into blackness. I climb the stairs and finally reach the desolate attic. Moonlight shimmers through a myriad of punctures in the gables like stars in a second sky, transforming wet wood into silver, and rice kernels, scattered over the floor to feed the spirits, into impossible snowflakes. As I slowly sink down amidst the beams, I feel that I am no longer in a dilapidated old building but in the depths of a breathing being. It is here, where the body of the last Raja once lay in state for seven days and seven nights of mourning, that the dark lips of the shadows finally break their silence. Instead of words what follows is a long whisper of relief that reaches my innermost being. The world outside no longer matters. Only here, in this forgotten corner peace prevails; it is only here that my existence burdens me no longer, my angst dispelled by communion with the House of the Raja.

EPILOGUE

Societies strive to keep memories alive because they feel the past defines what they are now, and that without those memories, they would go astray. While historical facts can be objectively recorded, the causes and consequences of each particular event is open to interpretation. Thus, history is constantly reinterpreted, distorted, revised or romanticised according to current realities. In some cultures and societies, historical memory has been suppressed, neglected or simply omitted for political reasons, creating an abnormal space that brings on a crisis of identity. I was drawn to the echoes and secrets of history in one of those places where past has been deliberately buried: Thailand's so-called Deep South.

The photographs from my trip did not try to document what I saw, but rather evince the wellspring of loss and solitude that moved me. When this body of work was exhibited in Bangkok and published as a photo book, I hoped it would reach other people's hearts and inspire empathy and foster interest towards a forsaken region that needed to recoup its dignity and the recognition it deserves as a cultural progenitor in Southeast Asia.

One morning, two weeks after the book launch, my friend Hannan called me in tears. Part of the House of the Raja had collapsed. It had happened all of a sudden, in the middle of the night. I immediately booked a flight to Narathiwat.

The Malay community responded to the loss with great distress, confronting the reality that their heritage was fading before their very eyes. An acrimonious discussion on how to safeguard the building ensued. TV channels took interest in the issue and journalists began pouring into town. People who claimed to know best about the building and what should be done scrambled to be interviewed, trying to earn as much credit as possible. Still upset over the fate of the house, Hannan preferred to steer clear from the spectacle that was underway.

Hannan picked me up at the airport and drove me to the House of the Raja, my second home in Narathiwat. He always received me with a broad smile, but this time he met me with concerned eyes.

"We have to talk," he said, making a stopover for a quick lunch at a humble roadside eatery.

After the partial collapse, things had developed quickly. The owners of the property, the alleged heirs of the late raja we had visited, told Ayoh-ha to leave the house. They deplored his rituals, remnants of an ancient Hindu heritage that, despite being part of the Malay culture, were deemed heretical by Muslim conservatives. As news broadcasted images of the derelict palace and interviews with local academics, the owners, probably feeling they were losing face, finally agreed to donate both the land and the building to the government to allow for its restoration. The Ministry of Culture's fine arts department sent architects to assess the condition of the structure and estimated a budget of three million baht for the project. Hannan, who bemoaned what he saw as yet another defeat for the Malay community, asked me bitterly, "How long did it take you to understand what the *Rumoh Rajo* is? Four years? They have given it away in just ten days…"

Arriving at the house, we found it enclosed by a makeshift fence made of corrugated iron sheet – the same cold, soulless pieces of cheap metal I have seen used so many times to replace the beautiful tiled roofs and wooden panels of old Malay buildings in disrepair. On the fence, someone had fixed a red board with a trespass warning sign. I paused, staring at the broken front of the building. Gone were the façade, the roof and its distinctive finial gracing the apex. Only the arched entrance and frame stood. A door to nowhere.

Hannan and I always spoke in Thai because it was the language we both could communicate best with each other. But this time, as we stared at the jumble of wood and clay in wordless dismay, he broke the silence in perfect English.

"I know this is the last time for you."

We climbed the temporary staircase that had been placed on the side to access the veranda, removed our shoes, and ceremoniously put them aside. Inside, all the doors were wide open. We picked our way across the roofless foyer, amid crumbled planks, beams and debris. Packed clothes, bags, rolled quilts and cardboard boxes with cooking utensils lay on the floor. Sitting at the back, where so many times I had listened enthralled to his anecdotes and fantastic stories, sat Ayoh-ha. I knelt down to greet him in the Malay way, clasping both of his hands and then placing my palms over my face. Then he embraced me. The powerful shaman sobbed like a helpless child.

I looked around me. The building felt very different from the last time I had seen it, somehow devoid of its mystical presence; even the light now looked dull and meaningless. This was not only a farewell to the house, but also a parting of the inspiration I found the first time I stepped inside. The edifice, no longer suspended in its own present, had returned entirely to the past as a mere historical monument. By the time it is restored, if indeed that really happens, the soul which had infused life into the House of the Raja will be long gone.

The couple whose crippled wife had been healed by Ayoh-ha came with a pick-up truck to help with the removal. I was glad to see them again. We all gave a hand to load the goods and chattels.

After a bitter farewell, when Hannan and I were about to leave, we saw an old man dressed in a dark suit who was sitting on a fallen beam. I was thrilled to learn that he was the author of the thesis on the house, but he would not address me. All he did was grumble about what had happened and about other things I could not follow. A man of his standing ought to be respected, so I listened in quiet rumination. My friend told me later that he was unhappy with me taking photographs of the property without permission of the family. Overlooked was the fact that his mother and brother had been aware of my work, since our first interview with them years earlier, without the slightest tinge of disapproval.

At that moment, Baeming arrived and greeted the man in black. His museum was doing really well, and was now open to the public as a cultural centre visited widely by people from other provinces and where students learned about traditional Malay arts in workshops. Even high ranking military officers would gladly host openings and folk fetes. Unlike my friend, Baeming was in agreement with the course of things.

"I know you are upset with all this. Me too. We all are. But we need to be realistic and if there is a way to save the house, this has to be the best one. Besides, Ayoh-ha has no right over the property. Sure, he was tolerated by the owners, but he should not have used it to his own benefit doing all that weird stuff."

Hannan did not respond. His attention was focused on the wreckage that the source of his inspiration had become. Baeming sighed and resumed his vindication.

"Honestly, do you really believe everything Ayoh-ha says? Come on. For a start, his mother is not 100 years old as he claims and his family has nothing to do with the Rajas. All those stories he tells are but fantasy to make himself important. Your father is an Imam. Ask him if what Ayoh-ha does is right, you will see what he says. You know that those things are forbidden in Islam, don't you?"

The word Islam woke Hannan from his stupor.

XAVIER COMAS

"Islam," he repeated. "Is that so? Then you must know that most of those artifacts you have in your museum are against Islam. For instance, your collection of kris. What do you think they are? Relics of animism and Hinduism. Why don't you just throw them all away? That would be in line with the Islam you preach."

"It's not the same," was the only response from Baeming.

Before leaving, Hannan vented his frustration in an outburst of anger, "I should just set the house on fire myself and finish it once and for all!"

* * *

Three years after those last bitter words, I visited my friends in Narathiwat. Faridah and Ayoh-ha lived in Kampong Takok, in a hut near the House of the Raja. They did not expect me. When I saw Ayoh-ha appear, lumbering out of the shack with his shoulders hunched, eyes lost on the floor, groping his way with his hands and his body half the size of what it used to be, I could hardly recognise the powerful shaman I had once met. He had been sick ever since he left the Rumo Rajoh.

Ignoring the trespassing warning, Faridah went there once a week to greet the spirits. She would sneak in and, after making sure that all was in order, she would remove the leaves that had accumulated inside and sweep the floor with tears brimming in her eyes. It sounded all too depressing for me to pay a visit, but Faridah encouraged me.

"Please, go. The house will be glad to see you again."

The makeshift metal wall had collapsed and vegetation was eating up the building. It was not surprising to see that the promise of restoration by the government had proven hollow. The house was dying and so were the people to whom it was bound. Bundor, the putative descendant of the Raja, died not long after our last interview. Tok Wae, the mysterious gentleman who revealed the house's call, had visited Hannan talking gibberish and faded shortly afterwards. Ayoh-ha's wife departed from her lonely life, and I worried that, sooner rather than later, Ayoh-ha himself would leave us too. This would surely be a devastating loss, for he did not just inhabit the building, but Ayoh-ha and the Rumoh Rajo were the same thing. One could not exist without the other. And like moribund souls, he and the House of the Raja had held on just long enough to allow their testimony to be imprinted.